Managing
Yourself
for the Career
You Want

The Results-Driven Manager Series

The Results-Driven Manager series collects timely articles from *Harvard Management Update* and *Harvard Management Communication Letter* to help senior to middle managers sharpen their skills, increase their effectiveness, and gain a competitive edge. Presented in a concise, accessible format to save managers valuable time, these books offer authoritative insights and techniques for improving job performance and achieving immediate results.

Other books in the series:

Teams That Click

Presentations That Persuade and Motivate

Face-to-Face Communications for Clarity and Impact

Winning Negotiations That Preserve Relationships

A Timesaving Guide

THE RESULTS-DRIVEN MANAGER

Managing Yourself for the Career You Want

• • •

Harvard Business School Press

Boston, Massachusetts

Copyright 2004 Harvard Business School Publishing Corporation

All rights reserved

Printed in the United States of America
08 07 06 05 04   5 4 3 2 1

No part of this publication may be reproduced, stored in or introduced into a retrieval system, or transmitted, in any form, or by any means (electronic, mechanical, photocopying, recording, or otherwise), without the prior permission of the publisher. Requests for permission should be directed to permissions@hbsp.harvard.edu, or mailed to Permissions, Harvard Business School Publishing, 60 Harvard Way, Boston, Massachusetts 02163.

Library of Congress Cataloging-in-Publication Data

The results-driven manager: Managing yourself for the career
    you want / Jim Biolos . . . [et al.]
        p.   cm. — (The results-driven manager series)
        ISBN 1-59139-346-9 (alk. paper)
        1. Managenent—Vocational guidance. 2. Career development.
    I. Biolos, Jim. II. Series.
    HD38.R414 2004
    658.4'09—dc22

                                                            2003021434

The paper used in this publication meets the requirements of the American National Standard for Permanence of Paper for Publications and Documents in Libraries and Archives Z39.48-1992.

Contents

Contents

Contents

Managing Yourself for the Career You Want

Introduction

• • •

The world of work is changing, and the old definitions of what constitutes a career have given way to radically new ones. In previous generations, managers expected to "climb the corporate ladder" by following a prescribed career path over the course of many years at the same firm. Today, most professionals can expect to change employers—and careers—at least several times during their lifetime.

People fine-tune their current jobs or switch careers for a wide spectrum of reasons. Consider these examples:

- Your current role is satisfying in some respects but unfulfilling in others. You believe that small-scale changes to your job responsibilities will enable you to derive greater meaning from your work.

- You've realized that, earlier in life, you embarked on the wrong career entirely. You wish to switch to a dramatically different type of work.

- You've followed the right career path for your needs for the past few years. However, new realities at your company or in your industry have forced you to make a change.

- You've changed as you've acquired experience and age in the work world. Now, the job that you previously enjoyed seems stale. Something's wrong, but you can't put your finger on what's causing your malaise. You're wondering whether a small change or major shift would reenergize you.

- You love your job, but it requires new skills that you must master to remain in that career. You need to decide whether you want to acquire those skills—or whether you'd rather change professions.

- You enjoy your work but have a poor relationship with your boss. Or you're uncomfortable with your unit or company's culture (for example, perhaps you tend to be introverted or shy, and you've found yourself in a group or organization that values aggressiveness and confrontation).

Regardless of where the impetus for career change originates—and whether we're fine-tuning an existing role or seeking a dramatically different one—we each need to think of ourselves as "free agents." Put another way, we must constantly evaluate how satisfying and meaningful we find our current work, decide what (if any) changes are needed, and implement those changes. We can't count on our supervisors to do this thinking and reconfiguring for us, nor can we expect our companies to guarantee us lifetime employment in the job of our dreams.

Management thinker Charles Handy agrees that we must take responsibility for what he calls "the pursuit of meaning" in our role at work. Meaning, he maintains, stems from three sources:

- Direction—the feeling that we're supporting a worthy cause

- Continuity—work that we believe will have a future long after we stop serving in that role

- Connection—participation in a community that we can identify with and help build

A meaningful career provides job satisfaction on several fronts:

- Financial—it supports you sufficiently

- Mental—it challenges and stimulates you

- Emotional—it provides a sense of meaning and belonging

- Practical—it meets pragmatic needs, such as location in a particular geographic area, proximity to desired community services, and so forth

Handy adds that the pursuit of meaning requires continuous learning. Management expert Peter Drucker concurs: Managers, he proclaims, must fully grasp what they're good at and what role they play in their organization. Moreover, they must continually assess what they'll need to learn to take on new responsibilities—which may or may not arise within their current work setting.

In other words, it's our responsibility—not our company's—to manage and build on our intellectual capital, as well as adapt to new challenges in our industry. To fulfill these responsibilities, we need a capacity for thoughtful, honest self-assessment and a willingness to keep our sights on the next possible stages in our career. We also need a predisposition for learning new concepts and skills.

Such continual learning can help us improve our existing work lives or find better ones. It can also benefit the companies that employ us. The best workforces consist of men and women who derive deep satisfaction and a sense of challenge, fulfillment, and meaning from their work. Think about it: If you don't enjoy your job, you have difficulty giving it your best. By contrast, when people relish their work, they generate valuable results for their companies. Managers and employees who love their work:

- Devote enormous amounts of energy to their job

- Go "the extra mile"—no matter how exhausting that added push might prove

- Embrace new responsibilities and challenges enthusiastically

- Dedicate themselves to their company and its goals

- Take immense pride in their performance on the job

- Feel a sense of community within the organization

Clearly, your ability to define and obtain the right career exerts a major impact on your own quality of life and your company's success.

So with these realities in mind, how can you, as a manager—assess your career and make any needed changes? The experts suggest *not* waiting until you're out of work (or miserable in a job that has somehow grown stale) to begin planning your future career moves. Start thinking *now* about what kinds of work you find most fulfilling and what changes may come along that may merit your attention.

Whether you've decided to reshape your current role or change careers entirely, the experts agree: Any form of career change takes courage, time, and patience—so don't go it alone. As you begin planning and then implementing change, continue honing your networking and relationship-building skills. You'll need mentors, support from others who are also actively managing their careers, and a thorough understanding of the workplace politics that influence who ends up in which jobs.

The selections in this volume provide valuable advice for navigating four major aspects of career management:

- Understanding the new world of work

- Exploring new professional identities

- Fine-tuning your current role

- Mastering networking and relationship building

Understanding the New World of Work

Yesterday's model of what a career should look like— namely, that old step-by-step climb up the corporate pyramid—is fast disintegrating. To manage your career, you need to familiarize yourself with the new models emerging in the world of work. In "Career Models for the 21st Century," Jim Biolos describes five models that have evolved over the past few decades. "The ranks of people pursuing [these] models," he explains, "include not only line managers in large companies, but also entrepreneurs, consultants, and solo operators. But most probably aren't aware that they have adopted one or the other."

Consider the models:

- **EXPERTS** define themselves by what they know. They spend their lives building expertise focused on a specific area—for example, direct marketing.

- **TRADITIONALISTS** strive for the "executive suite," mastering the political dynamics needed to achieve the ranks of senior management.

- **PORTFOLIO MANAGERS** pursue life voyages that include a variety of work experiences, skills, and accomplishments. They reach these by working for different companies at each stage of their careers.

- **PLANFUL ENTREPRENEURS** work in medium- and large-size organizations for some time, with an eye toward using the skills they develop there to eventually start their own business—often in a related industry.

- **SPONTANEOUS ENTREPRENEURS** develop a sudden passion for an idea and sacrifice the comforts of steady employment to build their own business.

People who embody any of these new models fluidly reshape their work within and across companies. They're free agents, relying on their own skills and expertise—rather than on a company—for their job identity and security. As quoted in "A New Breed of Work Force Demands a New Breed of Manager," Susan Gould maintains:

Free agents push their companies hard on how they can learn the skills to be competitive in the marketplace tomorrow; how to make global, cross-functional teams really work; how to master the technology now in place and the technological trends rapidly coming; and how to be rewarded fully and fairly for demonstrated performance.

Free agency raises new challenges for both managers and their organizations. For example, we must decide whether to place our loyalties more with our own profession or with our company. And we need to constantly look for ways to prevent ourselves from growing obsolete in today's rapidly shifting work world. Our organizations, for their part, must design new organizational structures—such as small, semi-autonomous business units—that can respond quickly to employees', as well as customers', needs. Time will continue to reveal how individuals and companies meet these challenges.

Exploring New Professional Identities

Whether choice or circumstances drive you to consider making a job change, you can boost your chances of a successful transition by taking a flexible yet thoughtful approach. In "Ten Steps to a More Rewarding Career," Rebecca M. Saunders presents a helpful road map. You begin your journey by managing the fear that may arise at the thought of making a major change. You assess problems with your current job and envision potential "dream jobs." Along the way, you network, weigh the pros and cons of changing jobs, and get the training and experience you need to demonstrate your worth in a new position.

But in "Changing Careers, Changing Selves," Herminia Ibarra warns against getting *too* mired in self-assessment and reflection. The most successful career transitions, she has found, involve "a messy trial-and-error process of learning by doing, in which experience in the here and now ... helps to evolve our ideas about what is plausible—and desirable." Ibarra recommends testing alternative careers you're contemplating now—and using the resulting experiences to learn about your "many possible selves."

How to implement the test-and-learn approach that Ibarra describes? Some people attend an executive-education program or take an extended vacation to explore new options. Others work on side projects with respected professionals or engage in volunteer work that exposes them to new possibilities. Still others request "stretch" assignments at work to get a sense of potential alternatives. All of these routes create a "bracket of time in which the rules are different and in which you're in different company." These experiences enable you to "try on" possible selves in a relatively safe environment, to see if there's a fit.

If you've recently "tried on" the role of manager or are considering doing so, the article "What You Must Learn to Become a Manager" can help. Author Linda Hill explains that individual contributors who become managers must navigate a difficult transition to a new identity. In their previous roles, they had responsibility for their own performance. As managers, they must develop others' skills and accomplish work through their direct reports and peers. Thus "task doers" transform into "people developers" and "relationship builders." Many new managers find this transition to a new identity surprisingly difficult—though coaches and mentors can help.

In "The 'Pay' from Volunteer Service Can Include Career Gains," David Stauffer explores a specific route to experimenting with alternative careers. Volunteering, he maintains, can "provide opportunities to gain skills and experience that translate into greater business success and bottom-line career gains." Stauffer lists numerous benefits of volunteering—including ways to learn more about management, a chance to master new skills required in the workplace, and opportunities to extend your professional identity. He also offers several cautions, such as avoiding overload and clarifying expectations about the time, money, and effort involved in each volunteering opportunity.

Like volunteering, taking on foreign assignments for your company can enable you to apply the test-and-learn approach to career change. But overseas postings raise unique challenges as well. For example, many families of managers who are working overseas have difficulty adapting to a new culture. In "Should You Take That Foreign Assignment?" Jim Billington recommends asking yourself four questions before deciding to accept an

overseas posting: 1) Does my company truly value foreign experience? 2) Does my industry truly value foreign
experience? 3) How much do I really want to work
abroad? 4) Can my family handle adjusting to a new
country?

Fine-tuning Your Current Role

Managing your career doesn't have to mean changing
jobs. It often entails improving the job you currently
hold—by setting new goals, managing your time and
energy more effectively, dealing more productively with
the emotions that can arise in the workplace, or getting
along better with your supervisor. In fact, thoughtful
fine-tuning in any of these areas can transform a less-
than-satisfactory job into a fulfilling, meaningful one.

In "Are You Ready for an Executive Coach?" Monci J.
Williams explains how to work with a coach so as to set
and achieve new goals. Coaching, she points out, "can
have real impact on a manager's performance." Most
"coachees" go through a process that includes an assessment of their current situation, the setting of new goals,
and "anywhere from three months to a year of sessions"
with a coach.

Though coaching can help you make needed changes
in your current work role, Williams recommends carefully considering the issue of confidentiality if you
decide to work with a coach. If *you're* paying the coach,

you can feel free to discuss anything with him or her. But if your *company* is paying,

> [a]sk for an up-front agreement about what the coach will tell your employer. Information appropriate to be shared includes the goals that have been set, whether you're showing up for your appointments, working toward your goals, and making progress. Inappropriate reporting includes personal problems such as depression and marital difficulties.

Like setting new goals, managing your time and energy effectively can vastly improve your work life. The article "Help for the Exhausted Executive: How to Manage 'Hecticity'" reveals that today's managers are experiencing "a whole new order of exhaustion"—thanks to advancing technology, globalization, and other changes in the business landscape. Performance targets grow increasingly tougher to meet, managers have ever-widening spans of control, and work goes on 24 hours a day. The consequences? People feel overwhelmed, helpless, and cynical.

But even the busiest manager can take steps to control "hecticity." For example, many practice relaxation and meditation at least once a day to tune out the roar of a hectic life. Others "place padding between appointments to anticipate the inevitable meetings or travel delays that might otherwise generate panic." A sense of humor can help you let off steam, as can "sanity time"—prescribed periods into which you don't allow work to intrude. Most important, a smooth-running team is critical to staving off hecticity, because you can confidently delegate tasks to members.

The article "Boosting Your Emotional Intelligence" adds management of emotions to the list of essential skills for anyone seeking to improve their workplace experience. According to Daniel Goleman, "EQ"—the ability to read, transmit to, and engage with other people—can play a larger role in on-the-job performance than IQ. After all, "intelligence and skills related to information are of limited use if we can't manage the human side of working together."

To hone your EQ, manage emotions through constructive internal dialogue; for example, say, "I know my idea is a good one" if the boss "shot you down" during a meeting. Know your "hot buttons"—how you react to the people and events in your work life. And develop a sense of empathy—the ability to read others' emotions. The payoff? As Goleman notes:

> Those who are adept in social intelligence can
> connect with people ..., [read] their reactions
> and feelings, lead and organize, and handle
> disputes.... They are the natural leaders, the people
> who can express the unspoken collective sentiment
> and articulate it so as to guide a group toward
> its goals.

"The Fundamentals of Managing Up" and "Are You Being Set Up to Fail?" conclude this section with guidelines for improving your relationship with your boss. A poor supervisor-employee relationship can sour even the most interesting and fulfilling job. To cultivate a trusting, positive relationship, find out how your boss views the business world. Does he harbor great ambitions or modest goals? Does she feel energized by hard-working subordinates or threatened by them? If you can't discuss such matters with your supervisor, speak with suppliers, customers, and other employees who know him or her.

Also, communicate in your boss's preferred style. Does he want information in report form or in spoken form first? Does she prefer high involvement in day-to-day operations or value delegation more?

Finally, watch for the "set-up-to-fail" syndrome, in which an unfortunate event (a missed appointment, a lost client) prompts a supervisor to question a direct report's performance. The boss starts micromanaging the individual, who begins doubting him- or herself and making more errors—confirming the supervisor's initial suspicions. If you've found yourself trapped in this syndrome, reverse it by discussing the situation with your manager. Find out exactly "what has gone wrong, what the boss wants you to accomplish, and when he or she wants it done." Then accomplish some tasks to demonstrate that you've fulfilled your commitments.

Mastering Networking and Relationship Building

Whether you're changing jobs or improving your current role, you'll need help from others. Networking and mentoring count among the most crucial resources for anyone seeking to better manage his or her career.

Though the case study "Can a Shy Person Learn to Network?" relates the story of a quiet executive who feels uncomfortable with what he sees as "schmoozing," the expert advice offered to the fictional character provides valuable lessons for any manager. For example, Herminia Ibarra recommends cultivating as diverse a network as possible and remembering that networking involves "give and take" rather than one-way assistance flowing from your contacts to you. To gather the information you need to make informed career decisions, Judy Rosemarin suggests clarifying in your own mind why you want to talk with a particular person before approaching him or her during a networking event. She also advises networking first with people you feel *most* comfortable with, then branching out to less familiar individuals.

In "Are You Ready to Get Serious About Networking?" Susan G. Parker shines the spotlight on formal networking associations or clubs. Though such groups vary, many share similar characteristics. For instance, to eliminate competition for referrals among members, they may allow only one representative from each profession. Many clubs meet weekly or twice monthly, and have formal rules about how they are run. And members are often expected to actively generate referrals for one another. Parker explains how to find the right networking groups for you, and how to both contribute to and benefit from membership in these associations.

Like networking, mentoring—in which more seasoned individuals provide advice and support to protégés—serves an important purpose in career management. In "Meet Your New Mentor. It's a Network," Jim Billington recommends that you cultivate relationships with three kinds of mentors: 1) *a company mentor*—someone within your organization with whom you can exchange ideas and knowledge about the firm, its industry, and its culture; 2) *a skill mentor*—an individual who has mastered your area of expertise and enjoys teaching; and 3) *a career mentor*—a person whom "you'd like to be in 10 or 20 years" and who "represents success as you define it, achieved in a career that you can realistically hope to emulate."

As with networking relationships, take care that your mentoring relationships follow the reciprocity rule. For example, even if you're junior in rank to your company mentor, you may possess knowledge (such as insights about "life in the trenches") that can benefit your mentor, just as his or her knowledge about company history or strategy can prove helpful to you.

The final selection in this volume, "Navigating the Succession Minefield," explores the political currents that any manager must understand and navigate while defining and working toward his or her next career move. Authors Dan Ciampa and Michael Watkins cite a series of political skills required for successful career management. For example:

- Build positive working relationships with individuals who hold the keys to the job you want.

- Help your peers succeed; you'll build "relationship capital" that may come in handy later.

- Attack problems that are important to the business; you'll cultivate your personal and professional credibility.

Though Ciampa and Watkins explore these political realities in the context of senior-level executives seeking the CEO position, their advice has merit for anyone planning the next step in his or her career path.

• • •

There's no doubt about it: Managing yourself for the career you want is demanding work. But by understanding the changing nature of careers, taking a flexible approach to job changes, knowing how to improve your current role, and mastering networking and relationship building, you stand a better chance of identifying—and achieving—the right career for you. You *and* your company will benefit.

Understanding the New World of Work

. . .

Definitions of what constitutes a career are changing and moving away from the climb-the-corporate-ladder model, which assumes that businessmen and -women have to log many years at the same company to advance in their careers. Today, people are likely to change employers and careers several times during their professional lifetimes. Moreover, we must now rely on ourselves—not our employers—to manage our careers.

The two articles in this section shed light on the new world of work. Through this material, you'll learn about five career models that have emerged in recent decades. You'll also discover guidelines for operating as a "free agent"—someone who depends on his or her own skills, expertise, and self-awareness to identify *and* achieve a fulfilling, meaningful career.

Career Models for the 21st Century

· · ·

Jim Biolos

At last count some 3,100 different tomes of career guidance competed for space on the shelves of U.S. booksellers. They offer counsel on everything from how to write a better résumé to finding the color of your parachute. The trouble is, most are premised on a single, increasingly obsolescent model of what a career should look like—namely, the old step-by-step climb up the corporate pyramid. Corporate pyramids aren't what they used to be—that loud screech you hear is technology and competition compacting many of them down to flatter structures, more akin to the roof of a Frank Lloyd Wright house. Careers have been transformed as well.

Nowadays, the whole notion of a career path, particularly one that proceeds with linear upwardness, is being called into question. Just as William Bridges, in *JobShift*, has argued that the 9-to-5 job won't survive as the mainstay container or structure for our work, so also have experts begun to explore new definitions of what constitutes a career. In the process, they are catching up with the real-world experience of many people who are already living their work lives according to patterns that look unconventional by most historical standards.

Charles Handy, in *The Age of Paradox*, offers perhaps the most expansive, hopeful new concept of a career, as the pursuit of meaning in one's role at work. The British sage argues that meaning will come to those who develop a personal sense of direction, continuity, and connection in their work. Direction, in his terms, is the pursuit of a cause. Continuity comes from choosing work that will have a future long after you stop—a legacy, as it were. You can achieve connection through the selection of a community that you can identify with and help build. Wonderful guidance this, but not always the easiest to put into action.

One implication for managers does seem clear though: The pursuit of meaning requires a process of continuous learning. Peter Drucker urges that managers in the new economy fully grasp what they are good at, what role they play in their organization, and what they'll need to learn to take on new responsibilities, which may or may not be within their current work setting. Once you acquire this knowledge, it is your responsibility—not any organization's—to manage your intellectual capital, continue to build on it, and adapt to the new challenges of management. To this end, it will help a lot if you can develop a healthy and enduring capacity for self-assessment, an ability to keep your sights on the next possible stages in your career, and a predisposition for learning new concepts and skills.

What those next stages may be, and what kinds of new competencies you need to develop, will depend on the nature of the career you pursue. Don't limit yourself to thinking just in terms of the traditional climb-the-rungs pattern. We've turned up at least five career models, ranging from some classics to a couple that have begun to evolve only over the last decade or so. The first three are based largely on research conducted by Michael Driver, professor of management at the USC School of Business, and Kenneth Brousseau, managing partner of Decision Dynamics Group. The ranks of people pursuing all five models include not only line managers in large companies, but also entrepreneurs, consultants, and solo operators. But most probably aren't aware that they have adopted one or the other.

The Expert

You can often identify someone following this course just by listening to him or her for a minute or two. He defines himself by what he knows and spends his work

23

life building his expertise. Often, people pursuing this career model have little interest in taking on general management responsibilities, viewing them as a diversion from their continuing accumulation of focused knowledge. Within an organization, such a person might be a direct marketing specialist, for example, constantly honing his skills in how to reach people more effectively, but with little interest in other facets of marketing. Outside a structured organization, you may find the model embodied in a public relations consultant, someone who devotes her time to becoming more expert in tailoring a company's communications, handling crises, and helping client organizations implement effective public relations programs. In both cases, the primary career decision is to accumulate, burnish, and put into use the mastery of a particular area or skill. Driver notes that experts are often driven by strong needs for security as well as for—no surprise—expertise.

The Traditionalist

These are the people in organizations who are striving for the executive suite. They're political, in the sense that they try to identify the career steps required to make it into senior management. Thirsty for achievement or power, such folks seem to thrive on a sense of being part of an organization and on the prospects of exercising substantial influence within the organization. In times of change and uncertainty like our own, the appeal of linear upward mobility and of well-defined roles and responsibilities make this granddaddy of career models particularly attractive.

On the other hand, the climb up the executive ladder has always been risky—many more attempt it than succeed—and that won't change; it may only become more dicey. As organizations flatten, the number of rungs—and top positions—has been reduced. Contributing to the danger is the fact that in this, more than in any other model, success depends on the organization and on meeting its standards. It also requires a kind of political savvy that many managers today say they aren't interested in developing.

The Portfolio Manager

Not to be confused with the people who manage investment portfolios, these folks pursue portfolio careers, life voyages that include a variety of work experiences, skills, and accomplishments. One of the newer career models, it takes advantage of some of the fundamental changes underway in organizational structure, employment needs, and collaborative work environments. The portfolio manager is typically motivated by a desire for personal growth, creativity, and, to some degree, independence. Her focus is on continuous learning, but of a more wide-ranging type than that pursued by the expert.

A woman we know in the shoe industry is a good example. She began by selling shoes in a retail store. A few years later, she moved into inventory management for a shoe manufacturer, understanding that this was a way to build experience in a corporate environment while learning some of the nuts and bolts of the business. Three years later, she moved into product development for another manufacturer, where she combined her education in shoe design with her retail sales experience to help build a line of shoes for her employer. Her responsibilities include managing the offshore factories that produce the shoes. She knows she'll stay in this job for only a few years and is already thinking about what her next position should be. At the same time, she is creating the option to start her own business, leveraging her broad base of knowledge about the industry.

She has built her portfolio working for different companies at each stage in her career and now is a highly marketable candidate for a senior spot within her current company or at another. The experts would laugh at her lack of expertise. The traditionalists would dismiss her lateral moves as directionless. She knows, though, that she's following her passions, planning her future, and learning new skills at every stage.

You get a whiff of the portfolio model in the proliferation of management training programs for newly minted MBAs—give 'em a little taste of just about everything we do. Less noticeable, perhaps, are the thousands of managers who actually have portfolio careers up and running, either within an organization or on their own. To spot the portfolio manager at your company, look for the person who's looking to learn all aspects of a particular line of business—how to make it, sell it, finance it, service it, and develop the next, improved version. Or, she may be the manager interested in learning different aspects of a particular corporate function—e.g., the strategic planner who wants to spend some time in marketing, then some in finance. Or, transcending a single organization, he may be an HR consultant who focuses on providing advice in the area of competency development for a few years, then shifts to advising on performance management.

Driver and Brousseau in fact posit two versions of the portfolio manager. The first looks like the one outlined above. The second takes a portfolio approach, but the new areas he transitions into tend to be unrelated. Folks pursuing this version look for variety and independence and often don't even think of themselves as having a career.

The Planful Entrepreneur

When *The Wall Street Journal* ran a front-page article about Wesley Sterman, an entrepreneur who spent his first 10 years out of college developing the skills he'd need to start his own business, it pointed to a career model that has been evolving for much of the last decade but is only now becoming a conscious, widely acknowledged approach to one's life work.

Planful entrepreneurs typically toil in medium- and large-size organizations, and may have been doing so for some time, but always with an eye toward using the skills they develop there to start their own business, often in a related or adjunct industry. They may often talk about their intention to "do something on my own." Some may not have settled on precisely what they'd like to do, while others take very deliberate steps with a clear new business goal in mind.

Such individuals can be tremendous assets to an organization, despite the fact that they don't plan to work there forever. They can contribute several years of enthusiasm and commitment. But many still feel reluctant to come clean to their bosses, since a less-than-life-long commitment to an organization remains politically incorrect in many industries. Nor do most companies have management systems and HR arrangements to accommodate the motivations of these folks. As the size of the average U.S. company, measured in numbers of employees, continues to drop, look for this model to become even more popular.

The Spontaneous Entrepreneur

Think of Richard Branson, Bill Gates, and Michael Dell. This model is perhaps the easiest to recognize but doesn't have the planfulness that we usually associate with the word "career." People pursuing it are passionate about an idea, enough to sacrifice the comforts that other models afford.

There may be spontaneous entrepreneurs percolating within an organization, ready to erupt at any time, but more often these are folks who know early on that they're destined to build a business—their own business—and who don't particularly value the preparation that an established organization can provide.

Built into much of the new thinking about careers today is the recognition that our lives will afford us greater choice on this dimension. Some time ago Peter Drucker noted that as our life spans have increased— many people can now expect in excess of five decades of productive adulthood—our chances have improved for having more than one career. Handy continues this line of thinking by suggesting that there is clearly a "post-executive" career—from age 50 or so on—that has not yet been clearly defined. Unlike tribal cultures and religious orders, which have clear roles for their elders and draw substantial value from them, the business world still too often fails to find ways to engage the energies of former executives and managers who still have a lot to contribute.

In fact, it may be overly reductive to think in terms of just two careers, one pre-50 and the other after. The portfolio-manager career model can be understood as representing the choice of four or five separate, but related careers, each lasting 7 to 10 years over the course of one's work life. Alternatively, some managers may spend a portion of their career following the expert model, but be inspired 15 years down the road to head out as spontaneous entrepreneurs. Fifty years ago, not many of us would have had the chance.

For Further Reading

The Age of Paradox by Charles Handy (1994, Harvard Business School Press)

"Career Pandemonium: Realigning Organizations and Individuals" by Kenneth R. Brousseau, Michael J. Driver, Kristina Eneroth, and Rikard Larsson (*Academy of Management Executive*, November 1996)

"Ideas Sire Many Entrepreneurs, But Some Follow Career Plans" by Stephanie Mehta (*The Wall Street Journal*, February 19, 1997)

JobShift by William Bridges (1994, Addison-Wesley)

"The Post-Capitalist Executive: An Interview with Peter Drucker" by T. George Harris (*Harvard Business Review*, March–April 1993)

Reprint U9705C

A New Breed of Work Force Demands a New Breed of Manager

• • •

Tom Brown

Split-second changes in the marketplace, corporate take-overs and mergers, and an unparalleled push for profits seem to have made the idea of managing people an exercise in folly. But with all the corporate turbulence—or perhaps because of it—a new pattern seems to be emerging. An evolving breed of worker—and manager—is re-writing the terms under which employees and employers can mutually thrive.

"A lot of companies have already done the easy things that make for a better functioning workplace in the '90s, things like flextime and nice work surroundings," says Susan Gould, coauthor of *Free Agents: People and Organizations Creating a New Working Community*. "The really hard pieces to the puzzle of how to manage in today's workplace are now being shaped by people who are looking for something completely different from the traditional definition of an employee or a manager."

The Free Agent Work Force

You're a "free agent," says Gould, if you realize that "you need to depend on your own skills and expertise for your identity and security, rather than on a company. If you're a free agent, you need a workplace that enables you to maintain your own ability to stay on the cutting edge." But free agents are not "corporate types," in the standard sense of the term. Instead of worrying about climbing the corporate ladder and dealing with a cumbersome hierarchy, instead of focusing on the nitty-gritty of a job description in the belief that jobs are permanent, the free agent carries a totally different agenda.

"I'm seeing lots of examples," Gould continues, "of people pushing their companies hard on how they can learn the skills to be competitive in the marketplace tomorrow, how to make global, cross-functional teams really work, how to master the technology now in place and the

technological trends rapidly coming, and how to be rewarded fully and fairly for demonstrated performance."

Eugene Harris, who directs human resource development and recruiting for U.S. Steel, says this new, entrepreneurial attitude "is pushing us in management to
constantly update our technology. It's forcing us to make
learning about all aspects of the company and the marketplace a constant, whether it's in the classroom, via
CD-ROM, or via on-the-job development. But it's good
pressure, created by people who are eager, interested,
well trained, and capable."

> Today managers must learn
> to see a different reality,
> speak the unspeakable,
> anticipate the future, and
> risk appearing unrealistic.

That doesn't mean that free agents are contented, of
course. Bob Rosner, the syndicated journalist who writes
the "Working Wounded" column for major newspapers
and the abcnews.com Web site, estimates that he reaches
six million readers weekly, and that 50 to 100 write him
daily for advice. "As I think about all my correspondence

for 1997, there were definitely some dominant issues. People writing to me are put off by office politics, the kind of 'idiotic' work situations lampooned by the Dilbert comic strip, and a work/life balance that is very out of balance.

"But," says Rosner, who has compiled his communications into a book titled *Working Wounded: Adding Insight to Injury*, "workers today are also zooming in on the new boundaries for corporate loyalty—whether to be more loyal to one's profession than to the company, how to increase one's slice of corporate profitability, and how to keep from becoming obsolete."

How Organizational Structures Must Respond

William E. Halal, professor of management at George Washington University and editor of *The Infinite Resource: Creating and Leading the Knowledge Enterprise,* points out that the emerging aspirations of people at work actually square neatly with the requisites for operating a global enterprise in the future. "In order for companies to compete tomorrow, they will have to be structured in smaller, semi-autonomous business units that can respond more quickly to customers who themselves have to operate in an increasingly complex and chaotic business environment. Therefore, workers who feel comfortable with jobs and tasks that have a short time horizon, that require full but short commitment, that measure achievement right away, and that allow people to be more autonomous than in the past—all of this is perfect for the new model of a company."

How Managers Must Respond

"The profile of the successful manager of the '70s and '80s will not be what's needed in the future," says Donna Martin, who has been head of human resources in three Fortune 500 corporations and is now in charge of international human resource operations for Monsanto. "In the past, managers often derived their authority from whom they knew, what they knew, and what their position and title was." But in order to be able to "help others live through the constant change that's part of the world today," she adds, "managers need to stop telling people what to do and start asking questions like 'What do *you* think?' and 'How can *we* get this done?'"

Listening Becomes Critical

Martin sees a big development opportunity for many accustomed to command-and-control management. "Managers must learn how to listen, how to be open and honest in authentic ways, how to show respect for individuality—and even how to be vulnerable. This is the management skill set for tomorrow's work force. I can point to older managers who have learned to excel at all these skills; I can also point to younger managers who desperately need to start learning."

Arguably, what's fast overtaking managers and workers alike is an organizational model built upon "membership," in which everyone is affiliated with what others are doing, thereby generating a common need to manage business in new ways. Says Jane Seiling, who wrote *The Membership Organization: Achieving Top Performance Through the New Workplace Community*, "Anyone managing today needs to recognize that there are voices needing to be heard. Older or younger, in every organization, there are people with knowledge and experience that they want to share. Managers must tap into these people in order to be successful, and they can't do that unless they start listening to everyone."

Sharing Power

Seiling observes that some of the best managers she knows are long-time veterans who have taken the sea change in employee-employer relationships as a call to growth. "I can think of one manager, aged 53, in a public utility now undergoing radical deregulation. He once said to me that he plainly didn't want his management career to wither because those managed weren't responsive to taking orders in a status quo marketplace.

"Admitting that he also didn't want to be taken out of his office 'feet first,' he recognized that the first thing that needed to be changed was himself. Like a lot of managers dealing with the new workplace, he found that the more leadership he gave away to others, the more he was seen as a leader himself; the more he spent time teaching others, the more he learned himself; and the more he helped others to be successful, the more successful his unit was perceived."

Leading Change

Seiling elaborates on what she sees as necessary for a manager to become a change agent, in the classic sense of the term. For managers to grow in their careers today, they must build skills in five areas: seeing a different reality, speaking the unspeakable, challenging the status quo, anticipating the future, and taking the huge risk of seeming to be unrealistic—willing to appear less than credible—because they are trying to create a dramatically different work environment. "It's a big switch from the traditional management model," says Seiling. "The good manager today must listen, influence, partner, connect, and effectively suppress his or her own ego."

The Secret of Workplace Contentment

Given the new breed of work force, manager, and workplace, it's fair to ask, Is anyone happy? Although organizations seem to have been in perpetual flux for the last

20 years, there *are* workers and managers who have adjusted well. Martha Finney, a veteran business writer, has taken as her mission learning from people who have found joy in their work. Traversing the United States by car, she has sought out individuals—in large and small companies, in nonprofit organizations, as well as self-employed people—who feel charged up about the work they are doing. "It's too early to draw conclusions about how these people are similar," Finney notes, "but a few 'truths' already seem to hold. First, despite the changes and difficulties we all face, those who find joy in their work stayed true to their personal values. If they derived joy from working with people, they made sure that this is what they did. Second, they didn't let hard times knock them down. Adversity was never a reason to get them off the track that they wanted to pursue in their life and work. And third, the people I've profiled so far feel profoundly and uniquely designed for the work that they do. Each felt driven by 'a calling.'"

Based on current trends in the workplace, managers will need to be integrators, not insulators; team players, not team captains; communicators, not commanders. For anyone managing today's work force—and aspiring to manage tomorrow's—the key question is, Do you feel *called* to that work?

For Further Reading

Find Your Calling, Love Your Life by Martha Finney and Deborah Dasch (1998, Simon & Schuster)

Free Agents: People and Organizations Creating a New Working Community by Susan B. Gould, Kerry J. Weiner, and Barbara R. Levin (1997, Jossey-Bass)

The Infinite Resource: Creating and Leading the Knowledge Enterprise edited by William E. Halal (1998, Jossey-Bass)

The Membership Organization: Achieving Top Performance Through the New Workplace Community by Jane Seiling (1997, Davies-Black)

Working Wounded: Adding Insight to Injury by Bob Rosner (1998, Warner Books)

Reprint U9805D

Exploring New Professional Identities

• • •

Just as definitions of what constitutes a career have shifted, so have strategies for changing careers. The authors of these selections propose augmenting the traditional job-change approach—by which you figure out what you want to do and then search for the perfect job—with a decidedly messier process known as the test-and-learn approach.

With this strategy, you experiment with alternative professional identities you're contemplating—for example, by taking on side projects, dabbling in new interests during an extended vacation, attending a course, or engaging in other activities that let you "try on" different possible "selves."

In these articles, you'll learn strategies for taking on the managerial identity, specifically, as well as gain insight into possible new careers through volunteering and taking on foreign assignments for your company.

Ten Steps to a More Rewarding Career

● ● ●

Rebecca M. Saunders

You say you've been wanting to change the industry or field you work in? You say you've always wished you had done something else, lived somewhere else, worked for a different kind of organization? Well, now's the time to do more than dream. Drake Beam Morin, the career management/outplacement firm headquartered in Boston, reports that today's ultra-tight labor market has made companies more and more willing to consider job candidates who are making career transitions. But even if you're not quite ready to make the leap, you may want to begin planning now, because you never know how long your current job will last. Don't wait until you're out of work to develop what Elwood N. Chapman, in his book *Be True to Your Future*, refers to as "Plan B"—that is, a well-thought-out strategy "to provide an immediate and exciting opportunity should the present job (Plan A) lose its luster or disappear."

Whether the career change is by choice or by circumstance, a successful switch depends on a series of steps.

1: Don't Let the Idea Frighten You

Everybody gets scared when they start thinking and talking about a Plan B, writes Chapman. They fear jeopardizing their current position. They fear they may find themselves committed to relocating, or to spending lots of money on education. But most companies recognize that managers must prepare for possible change. Some even report that people who explore alternative career paths become more assertive in their existing work and bring new insights into the workplace. So if they hear about a manager investing personal time in self-development, they welcome it.

As for fears about relocation, pay cuts, or educational demands associated with a career transition, that's up to you. It's your Plan B: if you don't like it, you don't have to do it.

2: Think About What's Wrong with Your Present Job

Sometimes people are in careers that are totally wrong for them. Pamela Cooper, an outplacement counselor for Drake Beam Morin, was in that situation—and found herself feeling sick heading to work each morning Fortunately, says Cooper, most managers escape such a bad fit before it has so dramatic a physical effect on them. But if you're thinking about changing careers, there is something wrong—for you—with what you're doing now. Determine what it is, so that you don't make the same mistake twice.

3: Envision Your "Dream Job"

Some people already have an idea in mind. Others don't. If you're not satisfied where you are but don't know what else you want to do, Cooper suggests asking yourself what you like about your job, or what you liked in earlier jobs. Brainstorming answers can help you understand what you're passionate about—and that, in turn, can lead to insights about an ideal career. What general fields are you interested in? Can you identify specific responsibilities within those fields? One in particular?

4: Clarify the Vision Through Labor-Market Research

We all may dream about the perfect job, says Dr. Duffy Spencer, president of Productive People (Westbury, N.Y.) and host of the radio show "Just Relationships." But too often our dream doesn't match reality. There may not even be a job like the one we envision. If it does exist, study of the job market—from Department of Labor statistics to professional journals and local job ads—may reveal that the job won't pay enough. But even before you consider matters such as pay and openings, says Spencer, you need to be sure that you really want this job.

5: Get Your Priorities Straight

Mary Lindley Burton, coauthor (with Richard A. Wedemeyer) of *In Transition: From the Harvard Business School Club of New York's Career Management Seminar,* points out that any study of the market should take special note of the issues most critical to you. If balancing work and family issues is important, for instance, you may want to avoid jobs that require 60 hours a week. Burton also suggests you question your assumptions about jobs and job markets. For instance, some people might think that a move to academia from business would put them in a more relaxed, benign work environment. As any academic can testify, that's often not the case.

6: Conduct Informational Interviews

Mico Zinty, previously with the University of Maryland's MBA Career Center and currently global best-practices consultant for American Management Association International (New York City), recommends that managers set up informational interviews to learn more about jobs they think they might want. Every job has a downside, and managers should talk to people who hold such jobs to identify their negative points. Ask questions such as, What is a typical day like? How much flexibility do you have in defining your job and in scheduling and pacing your work? How much time do you have to plan your work? Does your job require long hours and lots of overtime? Also, says Zinty, you'll want to check the skills and abilities required by the job, to see how good the fit is.

7: Network, Network, Network

Burton suggests managers make a list of "every responsible adult they know" and contact those who work in their areas of interest. Today's business culture, she

One Woman's Changes

Pamela Cooper, an outplacement counselor for Drake Beam Morin, is an authority in helping managers make major career transitions—based not only on her credentials but also on her experience.

Right after earning a degree in psychology she became the youngest professor at the University of Connecticut. While in college at Penn State she hadn't given much thought to a career, but she loved teaching and felt a professorship was a natural fit. It wasn't. A big part of the job included research, an area in which she wasn't strong. "I was a square peg in a round hole," she recalls. She had been teaching for three years when she finally admitted to herself that she was in the wrong job. The signs were hard to miss: going to work one morning, she had to stop her car to throw up.

points out, allows this kind of broad networking. Five or ten years ago it might have seemed strange to contact relevant people in your college's alumni database, for instance, but there's nothing odd about it today. Also, informational interviews can add fresh names to your network of contacts who can help you pursue your dream job. Chapman believes you have to become a "career information magnet"—not only meeting one-on-one with people in the field of interest but attending group

After some thought about what she liked and disliked about the job—in particular, she liked working with people—she decided to seek a position in corporate HR. One year of study, plus some time spent offering free consulting, landed her a junior HR position. When the department manager left six months later, she got his job, and proceeded to move up.

She left that company to become a full-time mother. The company was in the midst of a workforce reduction, and she had been asked to oversee the decisions. "The last person I terminated was me." Then the firm hired to oversee outplacement contacted her and offered her a subcontract. Once again, however, she had to choose between career and family when she and her husband adopted two young children from Russia.

After a year off, she returned to the outplacement firm, working three days a week, often from home. She is, she says, very happy with her new life.

events to find out what changes are taking place in the field and what roles you might play.

8: Determine the Pros and Cons of Changing Jobs

You should have a job while you are creating Plan B, even if it's only a for-the-time-being job. Unemployed? Spencer suggests you take any job available while developing the dream-job plan. If you are employed, she encourages you to stay that way and assess your current position by creating a matrix weighing the pros and cons of changing. For instance, assume you're considering leaving the business world to become a teacher. On the plus side, presumably, would be a greater sense of fulfillment. On the con side might be a major pay cut and the need to go back to school to get certified. One financial manager recently left a business in New York City, sold his home in New Jersey, relocated to his summer home in Maine, and became financial manager for the local school district. At 58, working for a company going through the stresses of reorganization, he saw the move as fulfilling his long-term dream of a simpler, more secure, more fulfilling life. For him, the tradeoffs were worth it.

9: Get Whatever Training You Need

Zinty recommends self-assessment tests to gain a fuller appreciation of your skills and capabilities. (One such product she highly recommends, CareerLeader™, is available on the Web at www.careerdiscovery.com.) If Plan B demands new skills, you have to figure out how to close the gap. Often what you need is what Chapman calls "do-it-yourself learning"—you have to undertake a home self-study program or enroll in a night program at a local college.

10: Be Able to Demonstrate Your Worth

Here's where Plan B comes to fruition—if you truly want it to. Your plan may lead you to another position within your existing company, or it may take you outside. In either case, says Burton, you need to establish in the mind of the person interviewing you for your dream job that you have the ability to make the transition. Zinty agrees: "It's not enough to say to prospective employers, 'I always wanted to be. . . .' During an interview for your dream job, you have to show the fit—to market yourself—in an effective way." In particular, Burton suggests you anticipate the kinds of questions you will be asked and prepare answers that show how your past vocational background or volunteer leadership has given you critical skills. For instance, a previous job may not have included budget responsibility, but you could point to a position in a voluntary group where you managed funds.

For Further Reading

Be True to Your Future: Achieve Career Success and Personal Fulfillment by Elwood N. Chapman (1988, Crisp Publications)

Plan B: Converting Change into Career Opportunity by Elwood N. Chapman (1993, Crisp Publications)

In Transition: From the Harvard Business School Club of New York's Career Management Seminar by Mary Lindley Burton and Richard A. Wedemeyer (1992, HarperBusiness)

Reprint U9909D

Changing Careers, Changing Selves

. . .

Deep in the American psyche is the belief that you can always reinvent yourself. But just what does reinvention mean? If, for example, it involves a wholesale identity change, is there no continuity in our personalities over time? And how does the change take place?

In 1999, Herminia Ibarra, a professor of organizational behavior at INSEAD, in Fontainebleau, France, began conducting in-depth interviews with scores of people between the ages of 31 and 52 going through midcareer transitions. Some of these career changes involved 180-degree shifts in direction; others constituted moves into closely related work. Her book, *Working Identity: Unconventional Strategies for Reinventing Your Career* (Harvard Business School Press, 2003), lays out the surprising conclusions her research led her to draw.

"Our working identity," she writes, "is not a hidden treasure at our core, waiting to be discovered. Rather, it is made up of many possibilities: some tangible and concrete, defined by things we do, the company we keep, and the stories we tell about our work and lives; others existing only in the realm of future potential and private dreams."

> For many, the introspective approach to figuring out who they are just doesn't work.

Conventional wisdom holds that you must first know what you want to do—with as much clarity and certainty as possible—and then use that knowledge to implement a sound search strategy. Ibarra's recommendations not only fly in the face of the standard career search advice, but they also hearken back to another bedrock American tenet: The pragmatist's notion that you are what you do. All too often, abstraction and introspection get overemphasized in the early stages of a search. Most successful career transitions, writes Ibarra, involve "a messy trial-and-error process of learning by doing in which experience in the here and now (not in the distant past) helps to evolve our ideas about what is plausible—and desirable." So jump into testing the alternative careers you're contemplating, she advises. The constant testing, crafting, adjusting, and shifting back and forth may seem highly disordered from the perspective of conventional career wisdom, but they are actually indispensable elements in the process by which the self is revealed.

In a conversation with *Harvard Management Update* and with Stephen A. Marini, Elisabeth Luce Moore Professor of Religion at Wellesley College, who specializes in the role of religion in American public and intellectual life, Ibarra spoke about these strategies and the conception of the self that underlies them.

Marini

A lot of your subjects seem to have fallen into what they were doing. When they started, they didn't really think they were going to be doing that particular job for 30 years. Then, 15 years later, they say, "Oh my God—this isn't what I want to do."

Ibarra

There were actually three kinds of people. Some never followed their passion because it didn't make sense or they couldn't make money doing it or their parents thought being a musician was flaky.

Most people, however, never made a choice. They didn't know if they even had a passion—at least, they never found one. So they kind of bumped along: "OK, I'll go to business school. Maybe I'll figure it out." Or "OK, I'll take a consulting job and then I'll see what happens."

Then there were people who made pretty informed choices—but then the context changed. A lot of people in the managerial world are in that camp. They really wanted to be in the business world, but then there came a time when companies were constantly restructuring and organizational politics seemed to become nastier. People began to feel that they had no control over their environment. All of a sudden, things didn't make sense.

Marini

Was that because the environment changed in a way that the individuals didn't anticipate or because the individuals changed in the process? In other words, was there a push or a pull for the people to make a career change?

Ibarra

Both. In every single story, there's a push and a pull. The push is completely insufficient, however: you can get more and more miserable, but if you don't have an appealing alternative that's getting increasingly better defined, you don't take the leap. And it's not because you're a coward or you're resistant to change.

There are lots of different possibilities for any one of us. Each person has to find work that is both appealing, in the sense of being challenging and fulfilling, and also feasible from the standpoint of: Can I make a decent living? Can it work with my family situation or geographic constraints or my physical disability?

HMU

So I guess the most important issue becomes, How do you work on the pull, make it stronger, make it inform your next step?

Ibarra

Those answers really escape many people. The way they often try to find them is through the model that I call plan-and-implement. This is the model advocated by most career coaches and career advice books: You gather data, fill out self-assessment questionnaires, do some personality testing. You do a historical interview: What jobs have you had? What did you like? What didn't you like? You also do a preference inventory: Do you like working outdoors? Indoors? Do you like detail? Big picture?

You pull all of that together and try to hone it down to a few areas you might be interested in. You do some introspection to figure out what's been keeping you from trying those fields in the past. Basically, the bulk of the work lies in this internal assessment of what you like and what went wrong, with the assumption that then you can just go out and find a match.

But my interviews revealed that such an approach breaks down in many different ways. First, people's careers are the result of a lot of things—some random, some parental influences, some peer pressures, some economic opportunity. It's not even clear that your past experience gives you the right data that you need to come to an assessment of what you were good at and what you enjoy doing. Careers often unfold by accident. There are some career possibilities that you just don't know about because you've never tried or because you've never been exposed to them.

> Going to an executive education program or working on a side project at night enables you to get out of your imagination and "try on" a possible self.

What's more, it's very hard to whittle all that internal assessment down to an answer—even if you know what your passion is. I heard a great story about somebody who had held many impressive positions. Her hobby had always been things having to do with flowers; her fantasy was to have a really upscale florist shop. So she took a minisabbatical and persuaded the trendiest florist in town to take her in as an apprentice, pro bono. But she soon discovered that the reality of that life just didn't do it for her. She hadn't realized that she'd have to be up at 4 o'clock every morning to go to the flower market. After a week, she knew that was not what she wanted to do.

Marini

There's something very American about the role of the imagination in this process of self-discovery that you describe. I'm reminded of Ralph Waldo Emerson, whose contribution to the philosophical debate about how to bridge the gap between being and doing was to say, "Imagine alternatives, then act." Once you imagine a different world—a better world—then go make it.

That debate is still very much alive today: as people try to negotiate their way in an increasingly multiplex world, they wonder whether the old structured approaches still apply. You've essentially highlighted that debate in the context of career transitions. And what's distinctive about your test-and-learn approach is the recommendation that people take action as soon as possible: Don't just sit there spinning your fantasies and allowing your imagination to reify your fantasy—move into some kind of actual experimental context.

Ibarra

Speed is of the essence in moving from making a list of possible selves to actually testing any one of them. If it seems that relatively few people make the career changes they dream about, it is because many just don't take the first step. Which self we test hardly matters; small steps like embarking on a new project or going to a night course can ignite a process that changes everything.

HMU

But when people start trying out all these possible selves and alternative careers, don't they run the risk of losing sight of who they really are?

Ibarra

People don't necessarily repress their true self; they just have multiple selves. So changing careers means changing our selves, but this is not a process of swapping one identity for another. Rather, it's a matter of reconfiguring the full set of possibilities. In any of us, there's a part that's very pragmatic and there's a part that's very creative, and there are times in life when we give more time and space and energy to one side than the other. But if it's in you, eventually it kind of bubbles up, and it wants some airtime.

You start by envisioning possibilities. That opens up the Pandora's box of "Am I really going to make a change?" Until a particular possibility jells, people need to explore. So they go a little bit further out to the edge to check things out. But they keep coming back to the safer, closer-to-home alternative until that other thing has crystallized; it's a way of making sure that this new possibility is really what they want to do.

HMU

You maintain that the time during which we move back and forth between possible selves is anything but a sign of our lack or readiness—in fact, it's the key to successful transitioning. Explain what you mean by the role of rites of passage and rituals in helping people negotiate this in-between time.

Marini

Rites of passage and rituals are very important. When most people think of rituals, they often think of something like communion. But you use the term to describe a process by which people move from a structured, stuck place, out into a free zone, where they can try on all kinds of different identities and experiences, and then come back out a little different.

Ibarra

The people I interviewed found things like going to an executive education program or going on an extended vacation, or even something like working on a side project with a couple of people at night, creates a protected bracket of time in which the rules are different and which you're in different company and maybe have some guidance—that is a ritual in and of itself. All these experiments can be viewed in psychoanalytic terms as experiences that create transitional space, transitional time, transitional figures. They allow you to get out of your imagination and to "try on" a possible self, in a relatively safe environment, to see if there's a fit.

Marini

It's not only the moving into a space or a place or a zone where things were a little different and you can try alternative selves—the payoff of those rituals is that they help you connect with other people.

Ibarra

All the research says that adults learn by doing. They learn in connection to other people; the old dichotomy between being and doing is brought together. One thing that makes a particular job or career appealing is working with people you really admire—people who inspire you to be the most you can be. With role models in place, possibilities that you actually didn't imagine become quite attractive and quite feasible.

Reprint U0304C

What You Must Learn to Become a Manager

An Interview with
Linda Hill

· · ·

In contrast to management treatises that concentrate on tasks and responsibilities, Harvard Business School professor Linda A. Hill's book, *Becoming a Manager: Mastery of a New Identity,* describes the profound psychological adjustment involved in morphing from star individual performer to competent manager. In a conversation with writer Loren Gary, she elaborated on the challenges one faces in making this transition.

What's involved in becoming a good manager, and how is your understanding of the process distinctive?

When I first started to investigate this topic, I discovered there's a lot of research about what managers need to know, but very little about how people actually learn to lead and manage. So I designed a qualitative longitudinal study that would create opportunities for new managers to speak for themselves about their experience. The study captured not simply the content of what they were struggling with, but even more importantly, how it *felt*.

Becoming a manager means coming to terms with the difference between the myth of management and the reality. When they first became managers, the people in my study were very focused on their formal authority— the rights and privileges associated with getting the promotion. But they soon discovered their new duties, obligations, and interdependencies. New managers soon learn that formal authority is a very limited source of power; their subordinates won't necessarily listen to them. And peers and bosses, over whom new managers have no formal authority, play an important role in whether or not managers succeed. Management has just as much, if not more, to do with negotiating interdependencies as it does with exercising formal authority.

As a new manager, you have two sets of responsibilities to learn. One is to manage your team. The other is to manage the context within which your team resides.

That means managing the boundaries—the relationships of your team with other groups both inside and outside the organization, and scanning what's going on in the competitive environment to make sure that the agenda you set for your team is appropriate.

New managers often narrow their horizons too much; they mistakenly think they should just focus on their teams per se. But, in fact, unless they look up, and around, and manage the context, their teams are going to have unrealistic or inappropriate expectations placed upon them. They're also not going to have the resources necessary to do their jobs. And because of what's happening in business in general, context management is becoming a much bigger and more complex job than it used to be.

Basically, in addition to acquiring team management competencies, you also have to change yourself. You have to adopt new attitudes, new values, and new world views if you're really going to be successful. That change in professional identity is what people find the most challenging. The feelings managers experience as they adopt these new attitudes and views have a tremendous impact on the evolution of their professional identities.

You describe this process as a psychological transformation

Right, and it's one that has two pieces. First, you go from being an individual contributor, who is relatively independent, to being a network builder. You also go from being a person who's very technically oriented—fairly narrowly focused—to being someone who's responsible for setting the agenda for the group. New managers have to start viewing themselves as responsible for determining the group's agenda. Now the capacity to actually come up with an agenda, to think strategically, requires a lot of learning. To set the direction for a group is a much more complicated process than people might think, particularly in flat, fast-moving organizations.

Seeing yourself as a network builder and also as a leader—these are fundamentally different ways of looking at who you are, as opposed to, say, the engineer who's working in the lab or the consultant who is not yet a managing partner in the firm. Becoming a manager means learning to frame problems in ways that are much broader, more holistic, more long-term. Understanding what your role is, how you can intervene, and how you can have impact, is a continuous learning process.

That's the conceptual element of the transformational task. What about the emotional element?

Instead of feeling free, smart, and in control, new managers feel constrained, not so smart, and out of control in the first months, if not the first year. They feel stretched. Their technical competence can become obsolete, so then what do they have to feel expert about?

They feel out of their comfort zone in terms of their people skills. And there can be lots of stresses associated with leading others.

> "Instead of feeling free, smart, and in control, new managers feel constrained, not so smart, and out of control in the first few months."

Some of those stresses stem from the fact that, like individuals, organizations are not perfect—no matter how much you restructure them or revise their policies and practices. Managers are essentially paid for dealing with the reality that you can't get everything exactly right; they are the people who have to deal with the trade-offs that come from not having enough resources, or time, or an imperfect organizational structure or incentive program. Adjusting to this aspect of the managerial role is a major part of the transformation.

Another piece has to do with how you get satisfaction from your work. How do you get your kicks when you're a manager or leader as opposed to when you had a doer role? As a manager you may be many steps removed from the outcome; your relationship to the outcome is often more ambiguous, and you rarely have the same instant gratification you get when the outcome is a technical one that depends solely on you. So in order to feel satisfied in your new responsibilities, you must learn new ways of defining success. You must learn to like seeing other people succeed, to like helping them succeed.

You think people can actually learn how to get satisfaction from these new ways of operating?

They can learn, and they also can discover. In my research I found that people had lots of surprises when they became managers, some pleasant and some not so pleasant. Things they thought would be satisfying weren't, and other things turned out to be thrilling. Some people hadn't realized until they became managers that they really enjoyed coaching, seeing someone else succeed—and that, in fact, they enjoyed it more than solving the problems on their own. I don't know if I'd call this learning. It's discovering new things about the self.

The other thing that happens is that as you get better at your new responsibilities, you get more of the results you want, and that can be quite satisfying. So in that sense I think there is indeed learning; there can be some changes in the way you actually get satisfaction from your work experiences.

Another major point in your book is that people learn how to be good managers through experience rather than through training.

I don't think you can teach anyone to lead. I think you can help people learn how to teach themselves to lead and manage. You do this by providing them with some of the tools that they'll need to capitalize on their on-the-job experiences, for instance, frameworks that attune them to the key issues in a situation. We have all kinds of experiences from which we learn nothing, or from which we learn the wrong lessons, because we don't know how to make sense of those experiences.

You can also help people be more self-aware. For managers to figure out the implications of their style on a given situation, they need feedback—not simply about what they've done, but also about *how* they've done it. To the extent that you can provide people with this kind of feedback, you help them figure out cause-and-effect relationships. You help make the link between their intent and their actual impact. From this, they learn to be more strategic about their day-to-day activities, modulating their behavior to produce the desired outcome. Moreover, they learn to be more strategic about their careers, choosing the work experiences most likely to bring about the growth and development they'd like to achieve.

Along with developing their introspection skills, you can help people learn to act in ways that make others want to give them feedback. Sending the signal that they're willing to hear what others have to say will get managers the information they need to make on-the-job corrections. Managers who are relatively open to feedback and don't become defensive find that others will want to mentor and coach them.

Interesting—most of what you read about this topic deals with *finding* a mentor.

And to me it's completely the wrong way to think about it. People often have very unrealistic notions about what mentors are supposed to do for them. The models we use for mentoring, such as the parent/child model, or the professor/student model, are inappropriate—because in fact the people you learn the most from are your peers.

In that crucial first year of being a manager, what are some of the flashpoints or watersheds that people should be on the lookout for?

One thing is having the appropriate expectations of what is going to, in fact, occur. We all know that there are certain mistakes that a person who's new is going to make, but most companies don't know how to acknowledge that. It's as if when you're new, you're supposed to do just as good a job as a very experienced manager.

Delegation, for example—it's a very tricky set of judgment calls. Often you read that new managers have trouble with delegation because they're control freaks. But actually that's a very small piece of it. For one thing, you are still negotiating the identity issue—getting out of the role of the doer and into the role of the agenda-setter. You are also trying to learn how to assess trustworthiness. To delegate effectively, you need to be able to make judgment calls about who you can trust. Still another big mistake new managers make is in thinking that getting the relationship right with each subordinate, one-on-one, is the same as having an excellent team. The collective is very different from the sum of the individual relationships.

Delegating, agenda-setting, managing the team versus the individuals on the team: Companies need to acknowledge that these are predictable trouble spots for new managers. Only then can companies start thinking about what kind of coaching would be helpful.

People are quite impoverished in most organizations with regard to feedback and coaching. This is really a shame, because as they go through a major transition they're most open to new learning. Those are moments when a supervisor's intervention can really make a difference.

What makes for good coaching?

There's no magic to it; rather, it's usually a question of whether someone is available to do it. A good coach provides supportive autonomy. What's very important, if you're the boss of a new manager, is not to punish mis-

takes that are fairly predictable. It's not that you should-
n't hold the new manager accountable—you should—but
you should adopt a joint problem-solving approach to
the mistake. What lessons can be learned so that it does-
n't happen again? A good coach also inquires about the
kind of feedback the new manager is getting. What is the
nature of the feedback and how is it coming to the new
manager? Answers to these questions give a coach a
sense of where the new manager's blind spots are—where
he's not picking up important cues, where he's not asking for help.

That's a very subtle thing: People have such different feelings about asking for help.

Sure, and some people know how to do it more construc-
tively than others. This goes back to what I said earlier
about being a good protégé. If you're a high-achievement
kind of person, you may be just the kind of person who
likes to solve problems on your own, who has difficulty
admitting there's something you can't do. A number of
the new managers in my study talked about their reluctance to ask for help. If you're the boss, you're suppos-
edly the expert. And if you're the expert, why do you
need help?

From this psychological standpoint, it's very easy to
understand an ambitious new manager's reluctance to
ask for help. The same holds true from an organizational standpoint: Subordinates don't want to hear that

the new person running their unit is feeling out of control, and doesn't know what he's doing. I'm not suggesting that new managers *should* run around admitting to everyone how out of control they feel. But they do need safe places where they can talk about these often overwhelming negative emotions. The issues of safety are huge. Asking for help has costs associated with it. Often new managers will be as reluctant to ask a human resources person for help as they will their boss. HR people tend to be quite connected across the organization, so managers worry that letting the HR people know about their difficulties getting up to speed might hurt their chances for a future promotion.

What is it that organizations can learn from people who are in the process of becoming new managers?

New managers are like beginning anthropologists: They're desperately collecting any information that seems relevant to their new responsibilities. As a result, they can bring a fresh perspective on things, they can ask the question that really gets to the core of the matter.

One of the things that people in my study said about going to new-manager training was that they got a much better feel for what the values of the company actually were by reading between the lines of what happened during the training. When I shared the new managers' insights about the companies' values with senior managers, they were shocked—either because the new managers' impressions, unpleasant as they may have been, were dead-on, or because senior management had inadvertently transmitted the wrong signals.

Because they're searching, new managers are very sensitive to the mixed messages that a company gives. Companies would benefit from knowing how new managers are reading those messages. It creates a positive feedback loop: If an organization understands how its messages and values are being misinterpreted, it can make constructive changes.

For Further Reading

Becoming a Manager by Linda A. Hill (1992, Harvard Business School Press)

High Performance Management (CD-ROM, 1995, Harvard Business School Publishing)

Reprint U9707C

The "Pay" from Volunteer Service Can Include Career Gains

• • •

David Stauffer

As any manager with a good benefits package knows, "compensation" from a job can include more than money. That being the case, evidence is growing that there can be significant compensation from volunteer community service: "pay" that comprises, first and foremost, intangible rewards such as feelings of satisfaction, accomplishment, enhanced self-esteem, and giving something back to one's community.

This article, however, will largely bypass these most prominent returns to focus on the increasing recognition that volunteer service can, in a variety of ways, provide opportunities to gain skills and experience that translate into greater business success and bottom-line career gains.

Although such considerations may at first blush seem a little too crass or materialistic for overt assessment, experts assert that "doing well by doing good" can produce wins all around for business people who volunteer, the agencies for which they volunteer, and—most important— the common good. For example, University of Pennsylvania psychology professor Martin E. P. Seligman, writing in his book *Learned Optimism*, says, "It is not necessary to undertake [charitable efforts] in a selfless spirit. It is perfectly all right for you to do this because it is good for you, regardless of its effect on the common good."

Career Benefits for Managers

The following career benefits are among the most common for managers who volunteer in nonprofit organizations.

1: More Ways to Learn Management

Research conducted by Harvard Business School professor James E. Austin indicates that many business executives who volunteer gain new and different management experiences from their community service. "Learning occurs in a low-risk setting," he says. For example, "a middle manager noted that many skills can be acquired in a risk-free way by sitting on community boards—and that this is a tremendous confidence builder."

Austin headed a 1996 study of the volunteer involvement of U.S. corporate executives—including surveys of nearly 10,000 Harvard Business School graduates and of 316 CEOs of Fortune 500 companies, plus in-depth interviews of more than 200 managers on the motivations and gains underlying their volunteer service. Learning opportunities are cited as an important practical benefit by accountant Susan Howe, whose volunteer involvement includes work for local and state associations of CPAs, her college alumnae organization, and a local health care agency. "A volunteer group provides a non-threatening atmosphere for practicing interpersonal skills," says Howe, senior tax manager in the Philadelphia office of Ernst & Young. "It's easier to take risks because less-than-stellar performance probably won't have the same consequences as in the paying world."

For Richard P. Lewis, M.D., longtime chief of the Ohio State University Medical School's division of cardiology, volunteer involvement in the American College of Cardiology "helped me learn how to manage people in a positive way, for example, by not being threatened by talent in others, and instead taking steps to help them develop it. I'm convinced that helped me win an important committee chairmanship and, in turn, become president of the college."

According to Dennis D. Lee, senior vice president and group executive for human resources at Wachovia Corporate Services in Winston-Salem, North Carolina, "Volunteering lets you see how others handle conflict, communications, and a whole range of problems and issues." Lee has served for five years as chairman of the American Red Cross Benefits Plan board of trustees. "You're getting an insider's perspective on another organization, seeing what does—or doesn't—make it tick," he explains. "It's a laboratory, in a way: you can follow a program or project from start to finish."

The introduction by the Red Cross of a medical insurance vehicle for retirees known as a Medicare HMO serves as an example. "I had wondered how our Wachovia retirees might greet such a plan," Lee recounts. "Seeing it rolled out and greeted enthusiastically by Red Cross retirees gave me some added confidence. Plus, I now have a template of action steps and communications that can contribute to a successful launch."

2: A Chance to Go Where Business Is Headed

Perhaps more valuable than learning management skills per se is learning the new skills required in the workplace. Writing in the newsletter *At Work*, consultant Bill Schmidt contends that "the nature of volunteering supports this shift to shared leadership. It engages people's hearts and minds, and they are strongly motivated to learn how to be involved in common purpose with others."

Tips for making the most of your volunteer service

In surveys and in-depth interviews conducted as part of research led by Harvard Business School professor James E. Austin, business executives who are active volunteers offered the following tips.

Get the right fit. Do you want a start-up group or a mature organization? Highly structured or looser? Struggling or stable? Big or small? Local or national or international? Identify your short list, Austin advises, then read relevant documents such as financial statements, talk to board members and top staff, visit service operations, and "get a clear idea of what they would expect in terms of time, money, and effort."

Manage your involvement portfolio. If you end up with "multiple involvements," as many executives do, "think of and manage these as a portfolio," Austin suggests. "One CEO categorized his involvements as the 'compulsory beauty contest,' where his presence was required

This collaborative style of leadership is often the only one that works within nonprofits, Austin found—and it is becoming increasingly important in for-profit companies as well. As one CEO told him, "It's leadership in an environment where people don't necessarily have to follow. It's these very characteristics that we are trying to nurture within the business."

by his company position, 'hands-on operational,' where he played a policy-making role, and 'entrepreneurial adventure,' where both risk and passion were high."

Don't overload. "Overextending leads to dilution and gets spread across the involvement portfolio, so that all suffer," Austin observes.

Lead from your strengths. Stick to the same standards of performance you hold in your paid work. That's often what nonprofits value most in their manager-volunteers.

Learn from experience. Though your business experience is welcomed, Austin says, "the often slower, consensus-building decision processes [in many nonprofits] may clash with your preferences and experiences. An executive told me it's good at first to say less than he normally would say and listen a lot more, then judiciously apply business experience."

Know when to leave. Your time is probably your scarcest resource—if it's not being used well, start looking for another place to volunteer.

3: A Good Way to Get Started

"For people just starting out in business, volunteer experience may be one of the few things they have to put on their résumés," says Yale School of Medicine postdoctoral associate Matthew J. Chinman. "In a nonprofit, an inexperienced executive might have a chance to run meetings, work on budgets, lead a marketing effort—assignments that might not yet be available to her in a competitive, for-profit business."

4: The Power of Empowerment

Studies show that volunteering conveys a sense of empowerment that spreads beyond the volunteer activities themselves to a person's career and home life as well. Chinman characterizes this empowerment as growing from "an increased sense of obligation, feeling useful, gaining confidence, and learning new skills; feeling good about helping others; gaining self-esteem and enhancing life satisfaction; and reducing alienation." Dr. Lewis suggests the same: "I think the greatest bottom-line benefit is an altruistic one. Working for the College of Cardiology means working for the organization that represents excellence in my chosen field."

5: Opportunities for Extending Vision

"Broadening" is a benefit of volunteering noted by everyone contacted for this article. Researchers and volunteers alike found that volunteer activities that are different from what you do at work provide valuable exposure to a more diverse set of individuals, perspectives, and problems. "By participating in a national organization that deals with national issues," concurs Lewis, "I was exposed to a very broad range of perspectives. I could come back to Ohio State and say, 'That's how we've done it here, but let me tell you how they're doing it somewhere else.'"

As important as broadening one's perspective, perhaps, is broadening one's range of activities beyond workplace and home. In an interview Austin conducted, a company president said that "his deep involvement as a board officer of the local ballet has been a wonderful life-balancing experience that has served as a source of affirmation during periods when he was having business problems."

6: More Diverse Forms of Diversity

Austin found that many managers named exposure to new and diverse people and perspectives as one of the top benefits of volunteering. "A CEO of a manufacturing firm said it's easy for a suburban, high-income earner to become incredibly isolated from the realities of daily lives and the political and community issues that affect his or her business."

That sort of exposure is cited as a key benefit by accountant Howe, who notes that "volunteering brings a group of people together who would not necessarily interact otherwise.... Exposure to people with different backgrounds and experience helps you realize that people are fundamentally more alike than different."

Wachovia's Lee sees benefits in working with managers whose paid jobs are with a variety of employers. "At meetings of the Red Cross Benefits Plan board of trustees, it's common to hear my colleagues say, 'Well, here's how we handled that at VISA,' or 'At ARCO, we did it this way.'" Austin says many of his interview subjects echoed this comment. "A senior vice president of Duracell International said he goes to meetings and usually comes back with more ideas. He said, 'We have some employees who have only worked at Duracell, and have had robust careers here, but no breadth of exposure.'"

7: The Outsider's Way In

Marketing professional Rob Ringer, with his wife and two children, transferred from the suburbs of Minneapolis to the small town of Red Lodge, Montana. "We quickly got involved in the Boys and Girls Club here," he remembers. "The key attraction was the needs of many kids whose families aren't very well off financially. But volunteering has also been a way to meet lots of folks, show we care about the community, and break down the invisible barriers of being viewed at first as an outsider."

8: Not Just Good—Good *for* You!

"Altruistic behavior is associated with good physical and mental health," says Stanford School of Medicine stress management researcher Kenneth R. Pelletier, M.D. In studying the backgrounds and lifestyles of 53 super successful leaders for his book *Sound Mind, Sound Body,* Pelletier found a correlation between altruism and longer life expectancy. "There's a chicken-and-egg issue here," he notes. "Does good health make someone more inclined to volunteer or do the good feelings from volunteerism aid health? That's unanswerable, but at least we know there's an interaction."

So Should I Rush into Volunteerism for Career Fame and Glory?

No. Although bottom-line benefits could certainly in themselves make volunteerism a smart career move, researchers and manager-volunteers agree that any such gains are secondary to the feelings of satisfaction in doing good for its own sake. "The professional benefits are great," says accountant Howe, "but the social benefits are tops."

Austin's research confirms that this sentiment is widespread. "Service is belief-driven," he says. "Belief in the nonprofit's mission is the top reason our respondents gave for volunteering, cited by 64%. The next-strongest motivator is giving something back to society, cited by 60%."

Yale's Chinman says the most valuable benefits of volunteer involvement should be those that are "purposive." These are the personal beliefs "that are aligned with the goals of the organization," he comments. "I can easily envision that business executive who, after spending the week concerned mostly with the company's financial picture, seeks more of a pure opportunity to do something for others." Nonetheless, he adds, this primary objective need not be without the accompanying career gains.

Any Other Cautions that I Should Be Mindful Of?

Yes. University of South Carolina psychology professor Abraham Wandersman—who with Chinman has conducted an extensive review of literature on the costs and benefits of volunteering in community organizations—advises careful consideration of "costs," including time, energy, and material resources. "It's as important to assess costs—'What will I give up to do this?'—as it is to assess benefits—'What do I stand to gain?' By doing this, you're better able to use your volunteer time wisely, increasing the benefits and decreasing the costs. And you'll be more attuned to affiliating with organizations that understand the costs of volunteering and seek to minimize those costs for the people who give the group their time, effort, and other resources."

How Do I Get Involved?

Depends. If you're not currently affiliated with any community group and wish to locate one that matches your interests, Chinman suggests contacting the local office of the United Way, or a similar federation of charitable organizations. "Many of these local offices run a voluntary action center, which acts as a clearinghouse for volunteer opportunities." Harvard's Austin advises "some self-reflection about exactly what kind of involvement you're interested in and what you would hope to get out of it. Then link into the nonprofit networks—perhaps first through colleagues who are already active volunteers. But if your interests are very specific and only a few organizations can be identified, you might approach them directly to ask about volunteer opportunities."

Matchmaking programs are increasingly operated by alumni associations and chambers of commerce, Austin points out. Examples include the Volunteer Consulting Group of New York and the Business Volunteerism Council, the latter established in 1992 by a coalition of Cleveland business and civic groups.

"If you don't believe strongly in the organization," counsels accountant Howe, "don't offer to serve as a volunteer." But if you believe in the organization, don't hold back. Howe describes a response that's been repeated in all of her volunteer experiences: "I found that if you take the first step by putting a foot in the doorway, most groups will soon throw the door wide open."

For Further Reading

"Community Service: More Rewarding Than You Think" by Judith A. Ross (*Harvard Business Review*, July–August 1997)

"The Invisible Side of Leadership" by James E. Austin (*Leader to Leader*, Spring 1998, Jossey-Bass Publishers)

Learned Optimism by Martin E. P. Seligman (1998, Pocket Books)

Corporate Volunteer Programs: Benefits to Business (1993, Points of Light Foundation, Washington, D.C.)

A Corporate Employee's Guide to Nonprofit Board Service by Carol E. Weisman (1996, National Center for Nonprofit Boards, Washington, D.C.)

Reprint U9808A

Should You Take That Foreign Assignment?

•　　•　　•

Jim Billington

Call it the new conventional wisdom: If you don't get overseas experience at some stage of your managerial career, you're probably not going to make it to the corner office in the ever more global 21st century. Just look at the CEOs of the Big Three U.S. automakers, the yea-sayers intone—all had major stints running offshore divisions. Or cast a glance at the survey done by Foster-Higgins, an international employee-benefits consulting firm. You might expect the finding that 57% of companies with more than 1,000 employees plan to add expatriate managers over the next few years, but would you have guessed that 72% of the smaller companies surveyed planned to do so?

In your case, however, and just possibly in most cases, the conventional wisdom may be wrong. Yes, Messrs. Eaton, Smith, and Trotman all did put in big time in Europe (in Trotman's case, in part because he was born and raised there), but arguably the car business is one of only two U.S. industries that has a decades-long history of valuing foreign experience. (The other is banking.) And for surveys, what about the one by Douglas Ready, a professor at the Arthur D. Little School of Management, which found that between 30% and 40% of American managers working abroad return home before the scheduled completion of their assignments—generally a bad sign.

Not to mention what may await you when you get back, particularly if you're in a fastmoving business like information technology. Charles Polachi of Fenwick Partners, part of a global consortium that does executive search in the IT business, estimates that more than 50% of information-systems managers who return home subsequently end up unemployed for as long as 12 months.

Making the Decision

If your employer offers you an assignment abroad, look before you leap onto the next plane to Prague. Besides the questions you would ask yourself before accepting any new position—including "How will it look if I turn this down?"—find out the answers to the following.

1: Does your company truly value foreign experience?

Some measures of its bona fides in this regard:

- Do many of the company's top management team have tours abroad on their résumés? Or did they climb the corporate ladder without ever straying far from headquarters?

- Does the company work hard to make sure that foreign assignments are a success? Signs that it does include substantial preparation beforehand, and corporate concern for the well-being of the entire family.

- Are overseas postings made systematically? Does the human resources department get involved? While in almost all cases the person recommending someone for an overseas posting is a line manager, at smart companies HR is brought into the loop. AT&T, Dow Chemical, and Motorola all help their most promising managers map out three- to five-year career programs and include consideration of foreign service as part of the plan.

HBS Professor Chris Bartlett offers a more sophisticated framework for assessing whether your company is serious about valuing foreign experience. He observes that U.S. companies doing business abroad typically fall

If You Know You Want a Posting Overseas …

Okay, you've decided that a foreign tour will be important to your career. Now how do you go about getting one? The experts recommend five steps:

- Tell your boss that you want to go. As simple as it sounds, too many people neglect to, apparently believing that the company in all its wisdom will divine their secret yearning or that it will offer an offshore job as a matter of course. If the occasion doesn't present itself normally, mention your desire in your next performance review.
- Do a good job at home. According to a survey of 50 large corporations conducted by International Orientation Resources, companies select employees for foreign assignments based on their technical expertise rather than on any demonstrated cross-cultural fluency. The most important jobs are given to people who have the best track record coupled with some perceived aptitude for work abroad.
- Learn about your company's international business.
- As part of (3), get to know your company's international team.
- Learn a language that would be helpful in a foreign assignment, and let your employer know that you've done so.

into four categories in their approach to international business and service abroad. Traditional companies like Crown Cork & Seal, he says, view foreign assignments as ambassadorial or technical missions—carry the word, or the latest technology, out from headquarters—and don't particularly value the learning that may occur from immersion in a foreign culture as a way of substantially improving their core businesses. Multinational companies like ITT view national subsidiaries essentially as stand-alone units, and take the somewhat narrow view of foreign assignments as steps on a career path to greater responsibility within that geographic area. Global companies, such as Boeing, which seek product uniformity with a minimum of variations across nations, will value the effectiveness of your work abroad, but not necessarily what you learn from an overseas assignment.

By contrast, a transnational company (think P&G) attempts to achieve both global efficiencies and local responsiveness, and will value what you can bring back from abroad to help educate the company. Such companies seek to leverage their worldwide learning, and offer the foreign assignments that will probably prove most rewarding, both professionally and educationally.

2: Does your industry truly value foreign experience?

Even if your company does, the business in which you've chosen to make your career may not. Remember all those IT managers who came home to a cold welcome. If your industry favors technical specialization over a general management education, you probably should rule out a long stint abroad. "If you want to become the world's leading expert on derivatives, stay in New York," advises Bartlett. "A foreign assignment is not primarily for technical learning, but for international learning."

3: How much do you want to work abroad?

Be honest. Managers who think of a foreign assignment mostly as a ticket to be punched rarely succeed once they get there. Choosing a country or language because it is trendy also suggests a lack of the necessary conviction. Sticking power born of a personal passion for the posting is what matters. "Choose a country that you love," says Bartlett. "If I were 35 today, I would want to choose a country that I was intrinsically interested it—say, one to which I or my family had some historic tie. And then I would try to treat that assignment as a way to learn as much as I could about how to manage internationally. And I would try to build a network of relationships in many countries."

4: Can your family handle it?

The majority of managers who return prematurely from overseas postings do so because their families have trouble adjusting to a new country, observes consultant

Ready. "A foreign assignment is often a time capsule," he says. "You and your family might be going back 40 years if you are working in a developing country. The adjustment is not just a matter of culture and language, but conveniences as well. You will need a great deal of support from one another." Which you ought to begin lining up from the very start, by bringing them into the decision making on a foreign assignment as soon as you begin contemplating it.

Reprint U9608D

Fine-tuning Your Current Role

• • •

Managing your career doesn't necessarily mean switching jobs. Sometimes simply fine-tuning your existing role and burnishing your on-the-job skills can turn an unsatisfying career into a fulfilling one.

The articles you'll find in this section provide guidelines for making smaller adjustments to your existing job and improving your range of skills. Specifically, you'll discover how to set new goals through coaching, manage your time and energy more effectively, boost your interpersonal skills, and improve your relationship with your supervisor.

Are You Ready for an Executive Coach?

• • •

Monci J. Williams

The age of customization, which has brought us the personal computer, personal trainer, personal shopper, and personal dater—formerly "matchmaker"—now offers the ultimate educational service for managers: the executive coach. In a trend that's been growing for more than a decade, individuals and companies are seeking the counsel of coaches with a mixture of zeal and trepidation that only career-shaking change in the workplace can bring.

There is no definitive count on the number of coaches practicing in the U.S. and abroad—by now, it may well be in the four figures—and no certification that guarantees quality or qualifications. In recent years, their ranks have been swollen by outplacement specialists looking for new work. If you're thinking of hiring one, herewith a brief primer on what coaches can do for you.

Why a coach? Managers in the flat and fluid organization of today can't get work done by giving orders; they must finesse relationships with people throughout the organization. For their part, organizations driving for productivity demand high, and consistent levels of performance from each employee. And today's increased focus on short-term results, says Robert J. Lee, a long-time coach who now heads the Center for Creative Leadership, has "eliminated the tolerance for insufficient and idiosyncratic behavior."

The growing presence of coaches in the business world also signals a major shift in organizational attitudes toward the management of employees. At least in some places, coaching reflects an enlightened recognition that people can grow and change. "The attitude used to be, 'That's just Joe. That's who he is,'" one training and development specialist says. "Now it's 'Joe has some developmental needs he has to address. How can we put Joe on a path to growth?'"

Because coaching can have real impact on a manager's performance—even more than training courses, many human resource professionals say—proactive companies such as American Express, Corning, Hewlett-Packard, Morgan Stanley, and Philip Morris have begun to offer private coaching as part of leadership development. But the bald fact remains that most managers who are selected for coaching are targeted because, in the non-blaming language of the trade, "something's not working."

Coachees go through a process that includes an assessment, the setting of goals for change and improvement, a plan for achieving those goals, and anywhere from three months to a year of sessions with the coach. The most thorough assessment is 360-degree feedback, in which the coach collects information about what Joe is like to work with from everyone around him—peers, bosses, and subordinates. The feedback session, in which the subject hears the results, often occurs off-site over the span of two or three days, and for good reason: Though coaches are careful to dish up the good along with the bad, there is nothing more disconcerting than meeting up with oneself. Says Kathryn Williams, a partner in KRW International, a coaching firm based in Winston-Salem, "Sometimes people get angry. Sometimes people cry." Then they get to work.

While 360-degree feedback may be the assessment vehicle of choice when the coachee is, say, a key senior executive who has no idea of the devastating impact his inability to trust subordinates has on productivity, it is only used in about 10% of coaching situations. The reason: It's expensive and soaks up the time of about 20 other employees per recipient.

Binders full of feedback data may help legitimize a business service that, in some eyes, may stray too much into the realm of the touchy-feely (and some justification may be called for when the price tag runs from $175/hour to 10% of the executive's annual compensation). But coaches say that most career pitfalls are predictable enough for the experienced eye to spot even without all the paper.

> Confidentiality is critical. Ask for an up-front agreement about what the coach will tell your employer.

As an alternative to 360-degree feedback, some coaches "shadow" their coachees, following them around and taking notes. For managers whose problems are less critical, even that level of assessment may be neither necessary nor cost-effective. Many coaches get feedback only from the boss who retains them; then they focus exclusively on working out the kinks in the coachee's relationship with that boss. Other coaches say they can size up the situation just by talking to the person to be helped. One is Marilyn Puder-York, a clinical psychologist in New York City, who is most often hired by individuals themselves rather than by their employer. "People have patterns of behaviors and beliefs," she says. "When they talk, I can hear their themes."

The simplest coaching situations involve fit: Josephine came from a rough-and-tumble culture that put a premium on individual performance and a macho stance, which may have meant yelling at the boss when he yelled. But her new job at Collegiality Inc. requires a more laid-back style. Or the move necessitating coaching may be not from one organization to another, but from one rung of the ladder to the next. Managers most often need help, says Kathleen Strickland, CEO of the Strickland Group, a New York City human resource consulting firm, at three points in their career: when they first ascend into management, when they move into senior management, and when they make it onto the executive team.

At each point the subtle rules and requirements for success change. "As you move up in your career, communications and relationships are increasingly important," Strickland says. "Most people don't get that. They're still hell-bent on performing." According to Lauren Ashwell, a vice president of training and development at Morgan Stanley, "New managers are successful as individuals, and now they need to manage through other individuals. It's not clear to developing leaders what they're gaining. They know, however, what they're losing—the lifeline to what made them successful."

Coaches can also help common personality types be more effective—and less irritating—on the job. The standout dysfunctions occur at both ends of the human spectrum: people who are aggressive, abrasive, domineering, and/or so task-oriented they don't develop good relationships with colleagues, and people who are introverted and shy. Coaches even act as the organizational equivalent of a marriage counselor, teaching people how to surface issues and resolve conflicts up and down the chain of command. "The conflict resolution in most organizations," says Kathryn Williams, "is abysmal."

Consider the experience of a 40-year-old banking executive whose hard-charging style didn't fly when he changed companies: "I had come from a fast-moving, results-oriented culture that embraced change—a very natural fit for me. This culture wants change, but is scared by it. It wants to be results-oriented, but it isn't yet. How you get there is still more important than what you do."

The discomfort of poor fit exacerbated natural tendencies that can irritate colleagues: "I became short, adamant, and was just driving things through. I was tense, stressed, and came across as aggressive and tough. I was missing what was going on in the room around me—interpersonal dynamics, subtleties that were important to getting buy-in on my ideas."

The key benefit of coaching was making the executive aware of what was happening. "You don't charge into a restaurant and say, 'I want food now! Serve me,'" the coachee says. "You can't do that in the workplace either." Or, as the coach pointed out, you can—but it doesn't work.

If you are selected for coaching, the attitude, as they say, is gratitude, albeit laced with a dollop of caution. You have, after all, just been handed a customized map of the road to success. And fortunate you are in the 21st century in the employ of a company that values you despite your flaws, and actually—*mirabile dictu!*—wants to invest in you.

Now for the caveat: Confidentiality is critical. Unless you are paying the coach yourself, you are not the coach's client. The organization is. Ask for an up-front agreement about what the coach will tell your employer. Information appropriate to be shared includes the goals that have been set, whether you're showing up for your appointments, working toward your goals, and making progress. Inappropriate reporting includes personal problems such as depression and marital difficulties.

If you'd like to hire a coach for yourself, contact the human resource professionals at your company or at the local chapter of a professional association like the American Society for Training and Development. Pick a coach who has formal education in psychology or organizational development as well as experience in the real-world dynamics of business.

While it may not be as challenging as performing brain surgery on yourself, coaches recommend not being your own coach. "It's very hard to know what we don't know," says Strickland. It's also true that, human nature being what it is, most of us tend to toss out the truths we most need to hear.

If, however, you have already been jolted into self-awareness, the Career Architect, a system that helps people create their own career development plans, may help you move along. It is based on ground-breaking research into how and why people succeed and fail conducted at the Center for Creative Leadership by Mike Lombardo, a former coach and trainer, and his partner Bob Eichinger. It's available in workbook and software formats through Lominger Ltd. in Minneapolis.

As for those of us who prefer the lovely cushion of oblivion that comes with believing the problem is always someone else, may this article introduce you to the possibility that you, too, might benefit from a dose of managerial self-scrutiny and growth. The days of sweeping everything under the organizational rug, including one's shortcomings, are gone.

Reprint U9610D

Help for the Exhausted Executive

How to Manage "Hecticity"

• • •

Sleigh bells ring. Can you hear them? Possibly not. Possibly you are instead tuned in to the ominous tick-tick-tock of the deadline clock: a plane to catch, a meeting to make, a report to get done, a train to be on, a conference to attend, a call to return.... The challenge isn't that today's workplace is hectic. The challenge is that it's hectic all the time.

If you think this is a personal problem, you are, of course, correct. (Who, after all, would know better than you—except, perhaps, your spouse and kids?) But it's also a productivity issue. Being able to live and work with the constant press of business demands—that steady, unsteadying state that Tom Brown, a management consultant in Louisville, Kentucky, calls "hecticity"—is a basic professional competency that many of us have yet to master.

Today's hecticity isn't quite like anything modern man has had to manage before. While the term "burnout" was popularized in the 1970s to explain the personal exhaustion that felled fast-tracked professionals, including those in the so-called helping professions, some experts believe that today's managers are experiencing a whole new order of exhaustion.

"We have changed what it means to have a job."

We know about technology, globalization, and the maturing of American markets, but we may not recognize the extent to which they have altered the nature of work. Says Christina Maslach, professor of psychology at the University of California-Berkeley and co-author of *The Truth About Burnout,* "We have changed what it means to have a job." Now performance targets become tougher to meet in each succeeding quarter and fiscal year. Managers have ever-widening spans of control. In the boundaryless organization, work goes on 'round the clock. Employees and colleagues are located continents

You Know You're an Exhausted Executive When ...

The following unscientific quiz was inspired by the opening chapter in *The Truth About Burnout*, by Maslach and Leiter, as well as the real-world experiences of managers. If you answer "yes" to more than half the questions here, you're in a bout with hecticity, and you need to take the kind of active steps we've described to turn the situation to your advantage.

When you hear the term "global economic chess game," do you see yourself as a pawn on the board?

Do you see technology as your enemy rather than an assistant that helps you get work done more easily?

Do you feel you are being micromanaged by a more powerful authority in the organization who never speaks directly to you?

Are your spouse and/or kids asleep when you leave for work in the morning, and already in bed when you arrive home at night?

Do you feel that, because of work demands, you can't commit to community projects or organizations you care deeply about?

Have you spent more time this year than last year wondering what it would be like to work for a company that has a fireplace in its conference room and a basketball court in its in-house gym?

away. A 9:00 A.M. teleconference scheduled to accommodate the time zone of counterparts in Europe requires the American manager working in the Central time zone to be on the call at 3:00 A.M. It's the same with customers. There's hardly a moment, it seems, when some vendor, subcontractor, or customer somewhere isn't expecting us to be up and "at 'em" and ready to go.

Walls fell down, leaving us in unboundaried lives. Companies must now be open for business at all hours of the day and night, and so must we be, too. If a manager's home ever was his castle, it isn't now. The post-dinner time zone has become prime time for e-mails, voice mails, faxes, and the rest of what wasn't done before we turned off the office light at the end of the day. (Who among us sent up thanks at Thanksgiving to the gods of technology for making our work so wonderfully portable?) Says Duane Trammell, one of the authors of *You Don't Have to Go Home from Work Exhausted*, "It's easy to see why many managers feel overwhelmed. The only way they can get it all done is to take the writing, reading, and reviewing of tasks home."

Michael Leiter, the dean of the Faculty of Pure and Applied Science at Acadia University, Nova Scotia, and Maslach's co-author on the burnout book, believes that the organizational and career consequences for those who can't manage a perpetually hectic work pace are potentially devastating. The feeling of being overwhelmed "takes the edge off everything you do." As judgment declines, ineffectiveness takes its place. Maslach sees an increasing number of managers who become overwhelmed by work—especially the kind that involves continuous people contact and juggling of tasks. They withdraw into behaviors that dampen productivity. Such managers "engage in distancing themselves from their work," she says. They become "cynical about the prospect that anything they do can make a difference." They seek to find ways to work less, or they lose time fantasizing about how they could get away with it.

Best practices of one who has mastered hecticity

"Ah, yes," you sigh. "Tell me something I don't already know." Very well (and not a moment too soon): There are a few highly evolved managers who seem to be "doing it all," at work and at home. They are sane. They are happy. And still they get it done. It may well be that they are genetically superior representatives of the species. But these managers have established a set of best practices for the management of hecticity that the merely mortal among us can put to immediate use.

Jerry Tucker, assistant vice president for Learning Solutions at GTE, coordinates the development of 110,000 employees in this $21-billion worldwide company. Tucker is on the road once a week, trotting off to Vancouver, Caracas, and many places in between. At times, 70 percent of his life is lived on the road. Tucker has given almost three decades of such service to GTE, yet he seems more upbeat and buoyant than ever. That's because he has developed a variety of techniques to keep burnout at bay.

Some of his practices seem obvious. Tucker has a packing system that includes a shaving kit and a set of already-matched clothes ready to go. "I can be heading for an airport in 20 minutes or less," he says. Having arrived at one of his many destinations, he may find himself waking up at midnight, wondering where he is. "Sometimes," he confesses, "I wake up wondering 'Am I late?'" But Tucker tunes out the roar of a hectic life by practicing relaxation and meditation at least once a day. "Even on a jet, I find that 20 minutes of focused mind-clearing can make a powerful difference."

Tucker is unapologetic about managing his calendar so that he has the time he needs, placing padding between appointments to anticipate the inevitable meeting or travel delays that might otherwise generate panic. "It also helps to cultivate a sense of humor so that when business pressures seem insurmountable, you can reach inside yourself for a sanity check," he says.

His biggest contribution to sanity on the job is, surprisingly, in the investment he makes in carefully managing his team. He checks in and communicates with his work team to ensure that it is always operating from common goals. "You can't survive in management these days without making sure that everyone around you is moving from an understanding of goals and priorities, because that understanding provides the momentum to do the right thing." Note Tucker's recognition that a smooth-running team is critical to staving off hecticity: He views team unity as a "base" for both the business and himself. "If a manager does not trust, does not empower, and does not delegate to his team, then the work will soon overcome even the strongest individual," he says.

Doing it all—just not all at once

Tucker plans for "sanity time" at home. He conscientiously sets aside periods in which work may not intrude, using them to be with his spouse, work with community organizations, and pursue hobbies. "Over the years, I have had lots of interests, from working in a nature center to fly-fishing to competitive clay-pigeon shooting. Instead of trying to do them all, which was impossible, I now rotate my interests, doing different things in different years."

In this Tucker has put into practice a recommendation of Acadia University's Michael Leiter. Overwhelmed managers, Leiter says, can get "out from under" by taking responsibility for managing the aspects of hecticity that are within their control. "Every manager must make choices," Leiter says. "If you feel that you are becoming exhausted, it's time to realize that whatever is happening in your life isn't working. Focus can only come from making choices about what you can do and will do."

It helps, says Ann McGee-Cooper, an author of *You Don't Have to Go Home from Work Exhausted,* to work in organizational cultures that make it "safe to fail and learn, appreciate people, and encourage synergistic teaming." (Yes, and a manager can dream.) But it helps more to recognize that, if we can't change the workload, we can change ourselves. And we can change what we do to make our work more manageable. That is the way to tune out the din of the deadline clock, and to be available, when sleigh bells ring, to hear them, and smile.

For Further Reading

The Truth About Burnout: How Organizations Cause Personal Stress and What to Do About It by Christina Maslach and Michael P. Leiter (1997, Jossey-Bass Publishers)

You Don't Have to Go Home From Work Exhausted! A Program to Bring Joy, Energy, and Balance to Your Life by Ann McGee-Cooper with Duane Trammell and Barbara Lau (1992, Bantam Books)

Reprint U9712D

Boosting Your Emotional Intelligence

• • •

David Stauffer

Have you trained and developed today? Have you dou-bled your load with seminars and reading that stuff you full of information about everything, from aligning incentives with strategy to the future of your industry? Is your head filled with the specter of the financial goals you must achieve—so much so that said head has no more room for anything else?

If so, you may wish to pause for a moment (just a moment) to consider taking a slightly different tack.

Many of us have labored long and hard under the misapprehension that the ability to inhale and process large quantities of information is the critical competency necessary for professional success. But emergent thinking about the qualities and competencies that make managers successful is zeroing in on a capability that may be even more vital: the ability to deal with feelings.

Oh! shades of bad lounge singers ("Feelings, whoa, whoa, whoa ..."), and aversions to general soft-headedness. ("Feelings? I've got numbers to make with half the staff I had five years ago.") Yes—but hear out this growing chorus of experts. They say that intelligence and skills related to information are of limited use if we can't manage the human side of working together.

Until recently, the idea that emotional or interpersonal competency is separate and distinct from IQ circulated mostly among executive coaches and psychologists. Such professionals, as well as human resource and training and development specialists, have long talked about something called "interpersonal skills," a broad, fuzzy concept that is the workplace proxy for what we used to refer to in elementary school with the phrase "works and plays well with others."

But what is it someone is doing when they do work and play so well? What's the behavior that expresses the skill? Modern management scientists—who are in the process of trying to pin down the elements of success the way a lepidopterist preserves and mounts butterflies—wanted to know. And now they want to share those secrets with us.

We are indeed dealing with a separate competency, says Daniel Goleman, the author of *Emotional Intelligence,* the 1995 book that became a world-wide best seller. The title of his book notwithstanding, Goleman prefers the term "emotional literacy," because it communicates the idea of distinct skill sets, as does the term computer literacy. He says this "EQ" is the ability to read, transmit to, and engage with other people. He first saw the signs of its importance in studies that tracked the careers of people who graduated from Harvard in the 1940s. The most successful were not those with the highest IQs, but those who displayed the greatest emotional intelligence, a discovery that has since been supported by a growing body of research.

Goleman believes that EQ can be learned, largely through the ongoing, individualized training of awareness, through which we gain insight into ourselves that we can then apply to others. He and others advise the practice of self-possession, civic-mindedness, and empathy. Goleman in particular is a believer in the practice of meditation; in addition to his work as a medical science writer for *The New York Times,* he upon occasion teaches meditation classes. For those of us who are mindful of the fact that the chanting of "om" has not yet been sanctioned as a critical workplace productivity tool in our culture, several authors have written books with nutsyboltsier, more practical tips for how to practice emotional intelligence.

Manage Emotions Instead of Suppressing Them

Those who would guide us to greater emotional intelligence are unanimous in proclaiming the futility—indeed, the possible harmfulness—of squelching our emotions. Instead, they say, our objective should be their appropriate management.

In *Emotional Intelligence at Work: The Untapped Edge for Success*, psychologist Hendrie Weisinger suggests exchanging a reaction to being put down in a meeting by the boss for what he calls "a constructive internal dialogue. Tell yourself, 'He's being unreasonable. I will not sink to his level. I will not allow my anger to show. I know my idea's a good one.' ... After the meeting, you would seek a solution to this problem of your boss publicly putting you down."

In such situations, Weisinger observes, you are managing the "components" of emotion—"your thoughts, physiological changes, and behaviors"—so they work on your behalf. Changing thoughts after the moment of arousal can make our feelings easier to manage. "Constructive internal thoughts can help slow down your physiological changes and behavioral actions; a diminished arousal level can help you gain control of your thoughts and behaviors; productive behavioral responses—deep breathing, for example—can help defuse destructive automatic thoughts and facilitate return to a comfortable arousal level," Weisinger argues.

Recognize Your Hot Buttons

Today, after a seemingly uncontrolled outburst of anger, joy, or other strong emotion, we may sheepishly admit to having "lost it." or "gone ballistic." In such instances, we would have been well advised, Goleman reminds us, to heed Socrates' ancient admonition, "Know thyself." That injunction, he says, "speaks to this keystone of emotional intelligence: awareness of one's own feelings as they occur." Awareness that trails expression by even a split second comes too late, because there is "a crucial difference between being caught up in a feeling and becoming aware that you are being swept away by it."

Weisinger calls self-awareness "the foundation on which all other emotional intelligence skills are built." He advises bolstering this critical skill with "some serious thoughtfulness and the courage to explore how you react to the people and events in your work life." The simplest, but perhaps most immediately productive, of several exercises he suggests is "asking yourself several times a day the following self-awareness questions: 'What am I feeling right now? What do I want? How am I acting? What appraisals am I making? What do my senses tell me?'"

Weisinger also suggests electing a kind of emotional mentor—someone who serves as your model for coping and responding. "This is the individual you look to when you need to know, 'What would my mentor do in this situation? How would my mentor feel in this situation?'"

If You're not an Optimist, Become One

If enhanced self-awareness and more skillful self-management are the foundations of emotional intelligence, the final building blocks are optimism and resiliency. They are essential for maintaining motivation and preventing burnout. Optimism, says Goleman, "is an attitude that buffers people against falling into apathy, hopelessness, or depression in the face of tough going." Although a positive or negative outlook is to some extent part of "inborn temperament," he says, "optimism and hope can be learned."

Cognitive psychologists agree (see *Learned Optimism,* by Martin E.P. Seligman, and *What to Say When You Talk to Yourself,* by Chad Helmstettler). They recommend "positive self-talk," the internal dialogue that supports a can-do attitude. This is what a manager should tell herself: "I can do this marketing plan. I've researched all the figures. No one understands the marketplace better. No matter what, I'll get the plan done." She will suffer less wear and tear and loss to productivity than the manager whose internal cataloguing of obstacles and fears causes paralysis.

Even the most buoyant among us have bad days. But resiliency, says Robert K. Cooper, co-author of *Executive EQ: Emotional Intelligence and Leadership in Organizations,* "can be renewed in any number of ways—by a run or a hug, a talk with a trusted friend, a few minutes of fresh air or sunshine, a healthy snack, some hot tea or your favorite music, or a rerun of *M*A*S*H* or *I Love Lucy*." A master of self-restoration, he says, was Albert Einstein, who with equal vigor pursued the passions of his life's work and his "non-work life." The latter "included such diversions as boating, going for long walks, standing barefoot on the university lawn, and pursuing mundane family tasks or childlike adventures. He valued what this did for him in terms of emotional and mental renewal, and he kept at it, even when fame came to him."

Read the Emotions of Others

Taking the energy to focus on a colleague's feelings may seem the way of madness when we are so hard-pressed to get things done. But people with high EQs do this as habit. This, Goleman points out, is the habit of old-fashioned empathy.

If we've lost the habit of empathy, say Robert K. Cooper and Ayman Sawaf, *Executive EQ* authors, we can relearn it through basic observation. Sounding a bit like a hypnotherapist planting a suggestion in the subconscious, they say, "See [others], and sense what they seem to be feeling. Notice their eyes and posture, their gestures and tension level. Listen to them talk ... you can then take these deepened perceptions into account when you interact with each group member."

Use Your Emotional Intelligence to Help Others Boost Theirs

An organization is built on the mutually interdependent web of relationships among the many people who are stakeholders in that organization. Weisinger believes that an organization's strength comes from the strength of individuals' relationships and that the strongest organizations are built by emotionally literate employees who help others become more emotionally intelligent.

The payoff for what seems to be a lot of touchy-feely work, Goleman and others believe, is clear. "Those who are adept in social intelligence can connect with people quite smoothly, be astute in reading their reactions and feelings, lead and organize, and handle disputes.... They are the natural leaders, the people who can express the unspoken collective sentiment and articulate it so as to guide a group toward its goals.... They leave other people in a good mood, and evoke the comment, 'What a pleasure to be around someone like that.'" Now that's productivity.

For Further Reading

Emotional Intelligence by Daniel Goleman (1995, Bantam Books)

Emotional Intelligence at Work: The Untapped Edge for Success by Hendrie Weisinger (1997, Jossey-Bass)

Executive EQ: Emotional Intelligence and Leadership in Organizations by Robert K. Cooper and Ayman Sawaf (1997, Grosset/ Putnam)

Reprint U9710D

The Fundamentals of Managing Up

• • •

Jim Billington

It's no better a use of time than polishing apples, say those who disdain the idea of managing up. Worse, says management consultant and author Douglas Smith, people (and cultures) can become so obsessed with managing up that they forget to manage out. "Your organization must move from focusing internally on the boss to focusing externally on the customer," Smith writes in *Taking Charge of Change.*

The effective manager, however, need not view these activities as mutually exclusive. A strong relationship between superior and subordinate makes work easy. Lack of communication, misunderstandings, and the passive-aggressive or avoidance tactics that sometimes result siphon off time and attention we might more profitably lavish on the customer.

And let's face it. Getting along with the boss is a survival skill—and in the age of flattening organizations, more critical than ever. So should you decide to more effectively manage your relationship with the man or woman in the corner office, here's what you can do.

The place to begin: Figure out who you're dealing with by looking through your boss's eyes.

Understand Your Boss's Mindset

"Until you know how the other person is inclined to see events and think about them, management ... is nothing more than power plays and manipulative acts," writes Samuel Culbert in *Mind-Set Management: The Heart of Leadership.*

Everyone looks at the world differently, a basic fact we too easily forget. Subtle differences can cause huge misunderstandings. So take time to gather information about how your boss looks at the world. Speak with other employees. Speak with suppliers and customers. Speak with friends. Does your boss see the competitive landscape as a zero-sum game, or does he spy an opportunity for more people to win? Does your boss harbor great ambitions or modest goals? Does your boss feel threatened by hard-working subordinates, or energized by them?

Any information you gather about how your boss frames his or her thinking and actions will lead to the understanding you seek. Says Norbert Aubuchon in *The Anatomy of Persuasion,* "Aim for a clear, verified idea of management's needs as management views them, not as you view them."

Communicate in Your Boss's Style

"Effective managers recognize that they probably underestimate what their bosses need to know." They also "make sure they find ways to keep them informed through processes that fit their style," say John Gabarro and John Kotter in the 1993 *Harvard Business Review* article "Managing Your Boss."

Peter Drucker divides bosses into "listeners" and "readers." Readers want information in report form so they can study before speaking with you. Listeners want to hear information first, then read a report. Some bosses want detailed background, others a minimum of detail. Similarly, some bosses want high involvement in day-to-day operations. Others value delegation. Others don't want to hear from you when things are going well, but may enjoy the chance to help rescue the situation when they're not. Don't bog down the delegator with daily updates. Give the reader a chance to read. And if that's not complicated enough, remember that most managers err on the side of undercommunication.

Learn to Listen for the Tacit Clues That Tell You Who Your Boss Is

To understand your boss's style, you must learn how to listen for both tacit and explicit clues.

In our rush to get things done, we become stingy with the time it takes to listen. That makes us less effective than ever. Most of us spend about three quarters of our time in verbal communication at work. Half that time is spent listening. But according to Tony Alessandra and Phil Hunsaker in *Communicating at Work*, when we are listening, we are only doing so at 25% effectiveness. So three quarters of what we hear virtually goes in one ear and out the other.

Ever find your boss, your colleagues, or your mate giving you a funny look during conversation? While this may be a sign that a large piece of lettuce is stuck between your teeth, that look can also signal that you would benefit from a brush-up on your listening skills. Alessandra and Hunsaker offer helpful tips for managing your attention.

Two kinds of listening will help you understand your boss. They both require energy and practice. The first is evaluative listening, which seeks to answer questions and then form judgments. The second is active listening: putting yourself in the other person's shoes, suspending judgment, and offering continuous verbal and non-verbal feedback. Active listening will be the key ingredient in understanding your boss. Active listeners promote active talkers. Empathy almost always encourages openness.

Understand Yourself

Gaining insight into your boss will be useless if you do not also operate from an understanding of yourself. What's your mindset and style? What are your goals? If you are a reader and your boss is a listener, you will have to communicate more verbally. If your boss is a non-communicator when it comes to both receiving and sending messages, or has become so as a result of organizational demands, you may have to find ways to cover what you need in short, clear interchanges that will help make him feel you are not slowing him down.

If your mindset is zero sum and your boss sees endless opportunities, you have the opportunity to grow. If your boss is a delegator and you are hands-on, you must find someone else to listen to all your details. On the other hand, by carefully describing your difference in style to your boss, you might open her to modifying her style so that it fits more easily with yours.

In assessing yourself, pay particular attention to how you view your boss's place in your own career. Gabarro and Kotter say subordinates fall into various gradients of the categories dependent and counterdependent. A dependent subordinate views the boss as someone who, by virtue of the role, is an aid to progress. A counterdependent views the boss as someone who is a hindrance to progress. The amount of closeness or distance you have in your relationship with the boss will be determined by your "dependency" predisposition.

Define What the Boss Expects of You

This is the nuts-and-bolts next step you tackle after you understand your boss and yourself. In a way, you are shooting for a consensus—or preparing an informal consensus document—that defines each party's expectations.

Some superiors will spell out their expectations of you in great detail. These expectations should include broad considerations (the kinds of problems the boss wants to be made aware of) as well as specific goals (projects that need to be completed, or interim updates you should provide along the way).

But while some superiors articulate what they want, most do not. If your boss will not detail these objectives, you ought to, in a memo. Send it to your boss for feedback and approval. A follow-up conversation will usually surface any remaining expectations your boss may have.

If your boss cannot stomach looking at expectations spelled out on the printed page, initiate a series of informal conversations about "our objectives," and what managers in software engineering call "roles and responsibilities." (Note the use of the bridge-building word "our.")

Define What You Expect of Your Boss

Subordinates shy away from this, but if you define what you expect of your boss, you may wind up with a happy surprise.

If you tell your boss that you need to touch base, say, every day for just five minutes to discuss progress, your boss might give you ten. If, on the other hand, you need room to complete a project without the interference of "the long wrench," you might provide pre-emptive reports that make clear you've got the tools you need. These reports will also make clear that you will ask for other tools when necessary. Over time, you may find that this process helps shape your hands-on manager into more of a delegator. (You may also find yourself curbing your own tendency to manage hands-on with your own direct reports, since you will have a new appreciation of how constricting too much oversight can be.)

When subordinates are afraid to define expectations with a superior, a communication or comfort-level problem exists. Neither will improve if you assume your boss understands what you need, insist that he or she "should" be different, or deny that your needs exist.

These steps will create the most important feature of your relationship with your boss: trust. So ...

Build Trust

"Trusting relationships are the bedrock components of managerial effectiveness," Samuel Culbert writes in *Mind-Set Management.*

Trust is a by-product of both understanding and congruency of goals. When you thoroughly understand what makes your boss tick, and can align your style and goals with hers, you can build a trusting relationship. Distrust springs from a lack of communication, a lack of understanding, or a lack of goal congruence.

By building understanding with your boss, you can minimize disunity, and maximize the alignment of goals. You will also optimize the benefits that come from mutuality, the key ingredient to any relationship that works.

For Further Reading

Communicating at Work by Tony Alessandra and Phil Hunsaker (1993, Simon & Schuster)

"Managing Your Boss" by John J. Gabarro and John P. Kotter (*Harvard Business Review*, May–June 1993)

Mind-Set Management: The Heart of Leadership by Samuel A. Culbert (Oxford University Press, 1996)

Taking Charge of Change: 10 Principles for Managing People and Performance by Douglas K. Smith (Addison-Wesley, 1996)

The Anatomy of Persuasion by Norbert Aubuchon (1997, AMACOM)

Reprint U9709D

Are You Being Set Up to Fail?

• • •

Constantine von Hoffman

You're probably familiar with the warning signs. Your boss—for whatever reason—seems to trust you less. He or she questions your suggestions, supervises your every move, second-guesses your decisions—or doesn't let you make any. Welcome to the club: you're being set up to fail.

This is the phenomenon described by Jean-François Manzoni and Jean-Louis Barsoux in their study "The Set-Up-to-Fail Syndrome," published in the March–April 1998 issue of *Harvard Business Review*. The two researchers interviewed 50 boss-subordinate pairs in four large manufacturing facilities. They tested their findings by surveying 850 senior managers from a variety of countries and industries. What they found was that managers all over the world "create their own poor performers" by setting employees up to fail.

The syndrome usually starts innocently enough. Sometimes the employee really does have a performance problem. More often there's a difference in "attitudes, values, or social characteristics" between boss and subordinate—and the boss *decides* the employee has a problem. However it starts, the syndrome follows a pattern. The boss increases supervision, hoping to show the employee the right way to do things. "These actions are intended to boost performance and prevent the subordinate from making errors," write Manzoni and Barsoux. "Unfortunately ... subordinates often interpret the heightened supervision as a lack of trust and confidence." Before long, the boss's apparently low expectations lead employees to doubt themselves. The boss sees the doubt and hesitancy as further proof that the employee "is indeed a poor performer."

Not Just Theory

Ask people about this syndrome and you realize just how common it is. Michael Backer, now a human resources consultant, remembers being on the short end of it working for an insurance company. "They decided I wasn't the right guy for the job," says Backer, who runs Salitube Inc. in Southborough, Mass. "The manager took an inordinate amount of time to breathe down my neck.... They put obstacles in my way, and then they'd want something done in a ridiculously short amount of time." When Backer was leaving the company, it only got worse. "They said, 'We're not going to give you a severance package until you've finished this project—even though you were incompetent to do it in the first place.'"

> Sometimes the employee really does have a performance problem. More often, the boss *decides* the employee has a problem.

The syndrome isn't limited to any particular segment of the work force. "I've seen it at all levels," reports Howard Adamsky, principal with the HR consulting firm Thinking, Planning, Doing in Stow, Mass. "I've had someone say, 'My vice president of marketing has been here for six months and isn't doing anything.'" What's more, it can begin the moment someone walks in the door to start a job. "I've done exit interviews with people who have been there 20 years, and they remember their first day. They started out on the wrong foot—the job was never explained to them, and what was expected was never communicated to them."

A common situation leading to the syndrome, says Adamsky, is when a supervisor expects someone to accomplish a task but doesn't give the employee the requisite authority. Surprise: the job doesn't get done. "If I give you responsibility, I must also give you the authority to carry it out."

What to Do

While most people are familiar with being set up to fail, few know how to cope with the situation. Adamsky, Backer, and Jean-François Manzoni caution that it may be hard or even impossible to get back in your boss's good graces. Still, they hold out hope:

Start Talking

"One of the alternatives is for the subordinate to trigger a discussion," says Manzoni, "in hopes that the outcome will be the same as if the boss triggered it." While it's a scary thing to do, you may be doing both yourself and your boss a service. "It's not so easy for the boss to bring up the issue," says Manzoni. He or she feels "the threat and the embarrassment" and may not know how to do so.

Are You Setting Someone Else Up to Fail?

Even the best manager makes mistakes. It's easy to become irritable and unreasonable with someone you supervise without knowing it. But once you realize you've been treating someone in a way that does more harm than good, what do you do?

According to Jean-François Manzoni and Jean-Louis Barsoux, there are five steps to follow:

1. Create the right context for a discussion about the problem.

Select a nonthreatening time and place, preferably off-site. When you set up the meeting, use affirming language; make it clear this won't be a one-sided blame-fest.

2. Both sides need to reach agreement on the symptoms of the problem.

The intervention has to result in mutual understanding of the areas in which the employee may actually be weak.

3. Both sides also have to come to agreement on what might be causing the weak performance.

Does the employee have problems in organizing work or time? Is she lacking in knowledge or capabilities? In this context, write Manzoni and Barsoux, "It is critical

... that the boss bring up the subject of his own behavior toward the subordinate and how this affects the subordinate's performance."

4. Both sides should reach an agreement about performance objectives, and about their desire to have the relationship move forward.

"Boss and subordinate must use the intervention to plot a course of treatment regarding the root problems they have jointly identified," the pair write.

5. Both sides should agree to communicate more openly in the future.

For the boss that may mean asking to be told when she says something that implies lowered expectations. The subordinate should ask to be told when he does something that aggravates or confuses the boss.

To be sure, there are some cases where a happy outcome just can't be reached. At that point, says HR consultant Michael Backer, it's time to develop a professional, respectful exit strategy. "Allow a reasonable amount of time to let the person look around for another opportunity. Depending on the job and the economy, that could be a month or three. If the person has any kind of work ethic, they're going to do what they can to look good going out the door."

Set Ground Rules

Once you and your boss have agreed to a discussion, you need to lay down some rules to make it work. "You want to sit down with your boss off-site. Have a cup of coffee in neither party's office," says Adamsky. "You want to say, 'I know you're not pleased with my performance—I need to know very clearly what the problem is.'" Essentially, you're trying to find out three things: what has gone wrong, what the boss wants you to accomplish, and when he or she wants it done. What you're doing at this point, adds Adamsky, is what your boss should have been doing all along. You are, in effect, managing the manager.

Accomplish Some Tasks

Next you'll have to prioritize your goals so that you can meet the boss's expectations. "Your objective is to do what you said you would do," says Adamsky. "Every time you achieve a goal, make the other person aware: 'I made a commitment to you and I have fulfilled that commitment.' That's how you rebuild your credibility." Manzoni adds three points for subordinates to remember during this process:

Work hard at maintaining your self-confidence. This is a difficult time for an employee; remember the things you can do and have done well.

Fight the urge to withdraw. There can be an overwhelming and understandable urge to withdraw emotionally and devote most of your energy to self-protection. If you do that, you'll confirm your boss's doubts about you.

Don't overreach. Don't try to do more than you actually can in an effort to get back in your boss's good graces. That's just setting *yourself* up for failure.

Don't Give Up

If asking the boss about your own performance doesn't work, says Manzoni, "ask yourself what the boss likes in Bill or Joe or Cynthia. Maybe you'll see, 'the people he likes are like X, Y, and Z, and I'm not like that.' Then you have a decision to make: to try and be like them or to succeed on your own terms." Another possible solution: bypassing the boss without going over his or her head. If you have worked successfully at other divisions within the same company, try talking to your former boss. He or she may be able to give you advice—or even talk to your current boss behind the scenes and alter his perception of you.

For Further Reading

"The Set-Up-to-Fail Syndrome" by Jean-François Manzoni and Jean-Louis Barsoux (*Harvard Business Review*, March–April 1998)

Reprint U9811C

Mastering Networking and Relationship Building

. . .

Whether you change careers or improve your current one, you'll need help from others. Networking and mentoring (cultivating relationships with seasoned professionals who can provide support and advice) provide you with important opportunities to navigate the complex human relationships and political realities that characterize any workplace.

The selections in this part of the book provide general networking guidelines, including ways to contribute to—and benefit from—formal networking clubs or associations. You'll also discover strategies for building a network of mentors—individuals within and outside your organization with whom you develop mutually beneficial relationships. The final article in the volume explores the political skills you must master to take the next step in your career path.

Can a Shy Person Learn to Network?

Answers from the Experts

* * *

Danny Bloom had heard the advice so many times that he thought he lived in an echo chamber: "Network now—not when you're on the street." His job as senior vice president for quality at a regional commercial bank certainly impressed his neighbors, but he knew all too well that bank consolidation was ripping out staff jobs right and left, with positions like quality czar often the first to go. The trouble was, Danny wasn't a schmoozer. He attributed his rise through West Winds Bank to hard work, not politicking or résumé circulating.

Indeed, in seven years he had moved from teller to VP of marketing, past lots of job-hopping MBAs. When the bank's president asked him to launch a total quality management effort, Danny had taken it as an honor. Within two years he had been promoted to his current position, but only after many nights and weekends sweating through formal training in quality practices. In the process, though, he'd become a true believer, with confidence in the idea that TQM could revolutionize service businesses just as it had done with manufacturing. Moreover, he had thought until recently, quality was a hot field.

Of late, however, he had begun to worry. He was 43, with a spouse at home and two teenage children approaching college. Although West Winds' results consistently came in way above the industry average, he knew that employment in commercial banking would continue to shrink in the years to come.

What bothered him most were the sullen faces at meetings of the Society for Quality Control. To him it seemed that this professional association had turned into a kind of downbeat job fair; more of his friends showed up shopping their résumés. "TQM is a CEO fad," one said. "I'm surprised your boss is still with it." Another advised him to go back into marketing.

But Danny enjoyed quality. He didn't want to return to a line job. The president had asked him to take on the job of quality improvement, and, until he had a different boss, that was what he would do. "I'm not a hopper," he told an executive recruiter who had called him. His wife, in the course of suggesting that he at least scout around to see what other opportunities were out there, gently volunteered that it might be shyness, even more than loyalty, that kept him from doing so.

In the past few months, the phone calls from headhunters had stopped. He wondered why. Compounding his confusion was the fact that he loved the small California town where he and his family had lived for the past 15 years, and he didn't want to move. Still, he felt uneasy. "Network now" kept ringing in his ear. "But how do I do that?" he thought. "And how do I overcome this damnable resistance to the whole idea?"

Advice from the Experts

Herminia Ibarra: professor at the Harvard Business School

Danny is taking a very limited view of networking, a stereotypic view, and one that is not going to be that helpful. The place to start is to think more broadly about his network, not in terms of what kind of strings he can yank to get a job offer, but rather, as the portfolio of relationships that would give him the resources he needs to continue to develop his career. And these will help him become a better professional in the quality field, and a better person in banking. He needs to figure out what is he learning that's new. How is he adding to his portfolio of skills? How useful is he to his company and his department as a result of the people he knows and the information that he is able to gather? His usefulness relates closely to his ability to know what other companies are doing with regard to quality, information technology—whatever might be relevant. In general, he must think about his network more broadly.

Too often people fall into the trap of naively dichotomizing the "what you know" from the "whom you know." The fact is, whom you know is going to directly affect what you know. We are in a very rapidly changing world, and the only way you're going to keep up is to know what other people are doing, and to pick up useful pieces of information from wherever it's available. It sounds like Danny is limiting himself. He lives in a small California town, with most of his contacts through a single professional organization. This sounds like a network that may be a bit inbred, given the way the world is changing.

As background, Danny should understand that people typically have three different type of contacts in their work life. The first is the task network, tied to getting the substance of your work done. For Danny, it's the people in the different departments that work with him on quality. The second network—and it overlaps with the first—is the career network. These are people who offer advice, guidance, and a sounding board for your own development. They can help you gain visibility, obtain stretch assignments, and open doors. We usually associate these networks with mentoring relationships, but people these days don't generally have one mentor; they have a set of people who are helpful to them in the development of their careers. The third network, again overlapping with the first two, is social—buddies at work, neighbors in the same industry. These networks are based much more on liking one another, and doing social things together.

In his thinking about the subject, Danny may also be overlooking the importance of reciprocity, forgetting how vital give-and-take is to networking. He seems to view networking as the superficial act of using people to get information about a job that he may want or need. So he's not doing the things that will make him a useful contact to other people—he's not looking at networking as a two-way channel in which he can provide something to the people he networks with in exchange for what they give to him.

Reciprocity doesn't mean that everyone has to be your best buddy. As long as there is a give-and-take, you're on track to a productive way of networking. But that doesn't mean that you talk only to people whom you really like, who share your interests and who are just like you. Often the people who are just like you are not the ones who are going to help you broaden and develop.

The more diversity you have in your career network, the better position you will be in to find out about opportunities outside your immediate social and professional circle. Therefore, it's critical to broaden out into places that you do not normally frequent. You will hear about things you don't normally hear about. And that will make you more useful to other people. It's not just a matter of what these contacts will bring to you. You will bring more to them.

Danny has fallen into a very common trap, staying too focused on his own company and his own function. My research suggests that this is a real mistake, and it stems from the fact that we like people who are like us, who affirm our values, and with whom we are comfortable. But there's a limit on how much we can learn from people just like us. You want to have some complementarity so that you can learn new things.

Susan Roane: author of *The Secrets of Savvy Networking*

I would advise Danny to get his head out of the sand. The ability to schmooze simply means that you're easy to talk to. One study indicated that 88% of us identify ourselves as shy. The question is how do we push through it. In fact, shy people often make good conversationalists because their eyes are never roaming.

There are several steps that shy people can take that will help them on social occasions. When you're at an event, act like the host; be gracious and interested. Have a planned and prepared self-introduction. Read the newspaper and have at least three things that you can talk about. When you're in the room, have a smile on your face and look people in the eye.

Allie Roth: president of Allie Roth Associates, a New York City career consulting firm

Danny should really look at his priorities, weighing his desire to work in a secure job and live in a small town as children approach college against his strong interest in TQM. If the quality program were eliminated, would he prefer another position at the bank (if available) or a TQM job somewhere else? He should ask himself, "What do I really like about TQM?" Perhaps it's the problem solving, or his leadership in launching a new "hot" project—talents he could put to work in another area. Danny is more than a "box" of marketing or of TQM; he has a whole range of marketable skills, interests, and abilities.

Danny may never be a great schmoozer, but he can begin networking by talking to people he trusts within the bank and within his circle of friends. If he is passionate about TQM, he should begin thinking of building his visibility outside the bank. I usually counsel clients to go with their passions and strive for meaning in their work; Danny's enthusiasm for his subject will come through and will sell him well. If he has skills in research and writing, he can write an article for a business publication or speak at a trade association meeting. That won't threaten his current job. To the contrary, his gaining a reputation for being a leader in his field reflects positively on the bank and would build his reputation within it.

Judy Rosemarin: senior career management specialist at Partners in Human Resources, part of the Arbor Group Inc.

The true form of networking is not about getting a job but about making and maintaining good human relationships that are held together by mutual interests. Looked at another way, networking is the act of gathering information in order to make an informed decision. Without this kind of information, Danny leaves himself ignorant of what is happening in the rest of the world—a world perhaps loaded with opportunities. If he is afraid of change, he is like most of us. He may need to look at times in his life when he had to make changes, and how, at the time, he might have handled the situation best.

To be sure, Danny's shyness may compound his reluctance to network. Shy people need to go about it very strategically and be fully prepared before they begin. He should draw up a two-minute description of why he wants to talk with someone and write it down. Then, since his wife is encouraging him to get out there, he can rehearse with her and role play the first couple of times. He should start out talking with people with whom he feels most comfortable; networking will become easier after he has met a few people.

Danny is a solution. Now he needs to go out and find the problems. That's not schmoozing; it's just good research.

Reprint U9609C

Are You Ready to Get Serious About Networking?

*   *   *

Susan G. Parker

Every other Wednesday at 7 A.M., Dan Valdez and the other members of The Alliance get down to work. The 23 members of this networking group, representing diverse businesses in Houston, are there for one thing and one thing only: to help one another generate business.

Networking groups like The Alliance have been around a very long time. Benjamin Franklin, a printer by trade, had a networking group that included a writer, a surveyor, and a shoemaker. The group met each Friday for many years to discuss politics, morals, philosophy, and "the promotion of our particular interests in business by more extensive recommendation," Franklin wrote in his *Autobiography*.

Networking groups are a more formalized method of generating business than are, say, networking events put on by an area Chamber of Commerce. While they vary, most networking groups have the following traits:

- Only one person represents a profession per group to eliminate competition for referrals among members.

- Groups meet weekly or twice monthly, with formal rules in place about how the clubs are run.

- Members are expected to attend a majority of the meetings and generate referrals for one another. If they do not, they will be asked to leave.

- Membership is generally around 25 to 35 to provide a broad basis for referrals without becoming unwieldy.

Quid Pro Quo

What sets these groups apart from other forms of networking is that members are explicitly expected to help one another. In fact, that is their first order of business.

If someone comes just to "sponge," he or she will be drummed out of the group quickly, says Wayne Baker, professor of organizational behavior and sociology at the University of Michigan, Ann Arbor, and director of research at HUMAX Corporation (Ypsilanti, Mich.). "What we've found through our research is that the people who are most successful in these groups are the ones who invest in other people's success," Baker says. "It will come back to them many times over."

At a typical meeting of The Alliance, one member gives a presentation about his business. While he speaks, other members fill out a sheet with names of people they want to refer to him for possible work. Then, taking it a step further, members arrange for meetings between the speakers, the referrals, and themselves. The personal touch goes a long way, says Valdez, who helps business owners revive flagging companies.

One member who provides payroll services had a client who was having trouble with his business. The member set up a lunch meeting for himself, the client, and Valdez.

"He understood the client's business better than I did, so as I was explaining what I do, he told the client how I could help him out," Valdez says. He says that the group has generated more than $100,000 in business for him since he joined in January 2001.

"The group probably brings me a minimum of 15% of my business annually," says Valdez, who is president of Sentry Group Advisors, a consulting firm in Houston. "It also gives me great comfort and confidence that I have a virtual sales force out there helping me build my business. If I have a full client load, I don't have time for marketing. So this helps me market when I don't have time to do it myself."

The Alliance, like other networking groups, has rules about who can become a member. Except for professions like the law, where numerous noncompeting areas of specialization exist, only one person can represent a profession. Members must be in a service business and work directly with other businesses, rather than sell to consumers. Each member needs to attend at least 60% of the meetings per quarter. Each must have lived in Houston for three years and be seen by other members as a skilled networker.

> "We want people to get to know each other. People do business with people they know, like, and trust."

In other words, each new member must bring something to the table. Members also must deal with mid- or upper-level management in their work. The point is to help fellow members get past the "gatekeepers," Valdez says.

The structure has paid off. The group has generated more than $3 million worth of business for the members since it began in mid-2000, says Valdez.

Giving a Boost to the Little Guy

Doug Vergith, a vice president at State Bank of Long Island (Jericho, N.Y.), became persuaded of the value of networking groups after a branch manager told him how one had dramatically increased her client load in a previous job. He has since paid the membership dues at networking clubs for five branch managers and two business development officers.

Vergith points out that his bank is a smaller financial institution that competes with the likes of Citibank and Fleet. It focuses on small to midsize businesses and seeks to distinguish itself by offering personal service to its customers. The best way to convey that service is through one-on-one meetings or word-of-mouth referrals, rather than large advertising campaigns, he says.

In the first year of joining a networking group, the manager of one bank branch brought in seven new corporate business clients—or one-third of all new business that year in that branch.

Iris Taibbi, who first suggested the value of networking groups to Vergith, says that she generates about 70% of her new clients from her group, a part of American Business Associates (Huntington Station, N.Y.), which professionally manages networking groups in New York City and Long Island.

Taibbi, assistant vice president at State Bank of Long Island and manager of the Holbrook, N.Y., branch, says she also learns about new sales approaches and common

Finding a Networking Group

So how do you find a networking group? Network. Ask people you know who are successful about the groups they belong to, says Donna Fisher, networking expert and coauthor of *Power Networking*. Networking clubs are either formed by a group of people on their own or run by a professional group, such as American Business Associates. Professional groups will charge higher dues, but they also offer built-in leadership and oversight of the networking clubs.

To create a networking group, Fisher recommends that you:

- Make a list of some of the key people you know in business whom you admire, trust, and would want to have in a networking group with you.
- Narrow that list to ten people, and then to five. Find five people who would be willing to build the networking group.
- Hold a meeting at which you make a rough draft of bylaws and guidelines. Have everyone make a commitment to the group.
- Ask each member to bring in two members over the next six months.

"The more structured groups work better," says Wayne Baker, professor of organizational behavior and sociology at the University of Michigan, Ann Arbor. "A good networking group will have specific rules and procedures to get people to work together. The ones that don't work as well are the giant schmooze-fests."

mistakes from other club members. "I always walk out of the meetings so motivated," she says. For instance, "I can tell my staff that other salespeople have a hard time remembering to follow up on potential clients. We really need to make sure we don't make the same mistakes."

Small-business owner Don Clerc is someone else who has seen a measurable profit from using networking groups. Clerc, who worked for 18 years at large corporations, had to learn about networking when he started his own home computer consulting business five years ago. He has since joined three networking groups, and his wife, who also works at the business, belongs to another three.

Clerc requires that his employees join networking groups as well. He pays for their time to go to meetings and have lunch with other members.

The investment of time and money has been well worth it. Networking groups generate 80% of the company's business, either directly or indirectly, he says.

Social Time with a Payoff

Donna Fisher, coauthor of *Power Networking*, says that these groups, in addition to the professional benefits they provide, perform an important social function as well. "There is a basic human need to feel a sense of belonging, to be part of something bigger than ourselves and have a place where we contribute and feel valued," she says. "We all need to feel connected with others."

Fisher has been a member of The Windsor Club, another networking group in Houston, for 10 years. Her group meets for breakfast every other week. At each meeting, members introduce themselves and acknowledge anyone in the group who has done business with them or referred business to them.

> Members in one club must deal with mid- or upper-level management in their work. The point is to help fellow members get past the "gatekeepers."

"We think it's very important that people express appreciation and gratitude for each other," Fisher says. "It keeps us connected. When we're acknowledged, we tend to want to do more of what we are acknowledged for. It supports the ongoing group."

Last year, on members' birthdays, all the other members told the person celebrating the birthday what they had learned from him or her that year. Someone in the club wrote it all down to present to the person.

Members of The Windsor Club are also part of smaller roundtable groups of five to seven people. These groups act as advisory boards for one another's businesses. At their monthly meetings, each member gives a brief update on his or her business while one gets the spotlight, giving a 30-minute presentation. It is a chance for members to bring up problems they are facing, such as marketing or difficulty with employees. Others in the roundtable give advice and feedback. Members meet individually with another member once a month for lunch. In addition, the group holds monthly social outings, such as going to the theater or a jazz club, having a potluck dinner, or taking cooking classes together.

"We want people to get to know each other. People do business with people they know, like, and trust," Fisher says.

Reprint C0302D

Meet Your
New Mentor.
It's a Network.

• • •

Jim Billington

Ah, your mentor. A gray-haired senior vice president who helps you navigate the rocks and shoals from account manager to CEO, right? Sorry. The traditional mentor-protégé relationship has gone the way of the mainframe computer—while it hasn't completely disappeared, it isn't nearly as common as it used to be. Reengineering, flatter organizations, and a lack of gray-haired senior vice presidents have all contributed to the decline.

So who will teach you the ropes and guide you through the sometimes tortuous labyrinth of your career? Increasingly, experts will propose to you the words "network" and "association" as a response. But it's hard to pour your heart out to a network, or to model yourself after an association.

Several thoughtful writers offer a sensible alternative: a network—but a narrow one—of mentors. One person within the company. One who has mastered your area of expertise. And one whose overall career path you find enviable. So how do you go about finding these three individuals?

To Get the Most from a Mentor, First Be One

It may seem impossibly cart-before-the-horse, given our cartoon notions of mentoring as a wise old hand helping along the starry-eyed young thing, but the best protégés have themselves been mentors, according to Floyd Wickman and Terri Sjodin, authors of the book *Mentoring*. While a mentor-protégé relationship can be an invaluable one for both parties, it requires, at least initially, a great deal more from the mentor than the protégé. You will be a better protégé yourself if you have been on the giving end. The authors offer four key questions that you should ask in choosing a protégé: Is this someone who will

- respect your time,

- take action on information that you provide,

- show respect for your gifts, and

- pass on these gifts to others?

These requirements are exacting, but they underscore a key point. Mentors have something to give. Protégés must appreciate the giving, enough to value the mentor's time and willingly share the mentor's knowledge.

Fear sabotages many mentoring relationships. Will your protégé outdo you? Will your mentor hold back key information out of insecurity? A good protégé understands and appreciates the cost of transferring knowledge from one person to another, and knows how to ease that transfer so that it does not cause the mentor to fear. The best way to learn this is as a mentor yourself. Your protégé does not have to be a more junior person in your company—it could be someone working elsewhere in your field, a recent graduate of your alma mater, or a young person you encounter in doing volunteer work.

As you gain experience as a mentor yourself, you can apply this experience to thinking about the criteria for choosing your own mentor. Wickman and Sjodin offer a 21-step process for identifying and recruiting just the right person. It details everything from researching the candidate's background, to making the initial call, to requesting a mentoring relationship. If this seems impossibly canned, it is. But the process is helpful; their brand of sequential thinking can help you organize your priorities.

The Company Mentor

In *7 Survival Skills for a Reengineered World,* William Yeomans vividly describes the twilight of the mentor of yore, someone two or three levels above, not necessarily with chain-of-command responsibility for you, who took an avuncular, apparently spontaneous interest in your career: "That esteemed higher-up, worried about hanging on to his or her own job, has little time or patience for giving others advice. Also, would-be mentors could be worried that they might lose their jobs to the younger and lower-paid people they are supposed to guide."

Still, you can find a company mentor. The key factor is eliminating fear on the potential mentor's part that somehow your learning will be his or her undoing. One approach is to find a recent retiree, someone whose influence within the company remains strong. Another is to look for goal congruence, an overlapping of your passionate interest in some cause or purpose and your potential mentor's dedication to same. In *The Power of Alignment,* George Labovitz and Victor Rosansky cite a good example—unrelated to mentoring—of how alignment of goals can drive out fear in an organization: In the development of Ford's 1983 Thunderbird, the clear goal of making a car that any employee would be proud to drive overcame turf jealousy and bureaucratic infighting.

Company-supported mentoring programs, while a tad forced compared to the traditional evolution of such relationships, also promote alignment. According to Wickman and Sjodin, a study of 2,400 life insurance agents showed that mentoring improved productivity and success rates among new hires, while not adversely affecting the success rates of the mentors.

Besides the satisfaction of helping someone along, the possibility that he or she will learn something provides another incentive for someone to be your mentor. Although junior in rank, you might have significant, and up-to-date, knowledge that can benefit a senior manager. In addition to their technical skills, junior employees also have insights into life "in the trenches" that can benefit higher-ups in the organization. What you should aspire to in a mentor-protégé relationship is a partnership, rather than a one-way exercise in knowledge extraction.

The Skill Mentor

A skill mentor will help you forge your expertise in a particular functional area, and keep it honed. This person may or may not work for your company, or industry, but will possess a higher level of functional expertise than you have. The relationship will not be as intense as that with a company mentor, but should last longer. Since the principal sorts of satisfaction for this kind of mentor will be helping someone else succeed while advancing the discipline, he or she must place great value on teaching. Along the way, the mentor will benefit from having to keep current in functional expertise, in order to teach. In this case, too, the mentor must feel secure enough in his own career path not to be threatened by yours.

Trade and professional groups provide an ideal place to find such a mentor, and give the two of you a reason to meet periodically. Relationships formed in business school can also provide this kind of mentoring. William Hendricks, author of *Coaching, Mentoring, and Managing,* suggests the concept of "group mentors"—the mentor not as a person but as a series of associations you develop that build your skills.

The Career Mentor

Since in all likelihood you will change companies at least once in your career, and possibly change functions as well, it helps to have a career mentor—in the sense we're using it, an ideal or lodestar that you can look to as you chart your professional direction. This is the person that you, in your work life, would like to be in 10 or 20 years. The mentor may be in your industry or another, in your functional area or not. The critical point is that he or she must represent success as you define it, achieved in a career that you can realistically hope to emulate.

Choosing this person requires the most thought, well beyond the lists of steps offered in the books under discussion. You must define success, which means figuring out what you most value, and then try to find someone who embodies that success. Identifying that person, and persuading him or her to counsel you, could be the most critical form of alignment that you will undertake in your career. Obviously you need to find someone who sincerely wants to provide this kind of mentoring. The benefit to the mentor is not knowledge exchange, but rather the psychic rewards that come from leaving a legacy. Among the places you might look for such a person is the Service Corps of Retired Executives (SCORE), which is headquartered in Washington, DC. SCORE offers a formal and structured mentoring program for business people.

Although mentors are not easy to find these days, they still can be an invaluable asset to your career. Don't pin all your hopes on one. But don't seek out too many. One mentor in your company, another in your field, and a third in your career together can form the narrow, but broadening, network that you need.

For Further Reading

Coaching, Mentoring and Managing by William Hendricks (1996, Career Press)

Mentoring by Floyd Wickman and Terri Sjodin (1997, McGraw-Hill)

The Power of Alignment by George Labovitz and Victor Rosansky (1997, John Wiley & Sons)

7 Survival Skills for a Reengineered World by William N. Yeomans (1996, Dutton)

Reprint U9708A

Navigating the Succession Minefield

· · ·

Dan Ciampa and Michael Watkins

One minute he's the highly regarded #2 executive, ready to lead the company when the CEO steps down. The next minute he's been fired, or has left "to pursue other opportunities."

What went wrong? Recent high-profile examples of the premature departure of a second-in-command underscore what the research shows: of the executives promoted from within to the #2 spot and expecting to succeed the CEO, half never make it to the top, leaving their companies within five years. Even more startling is the success rate for people coming into #2 positions from the outside: after five years, only 24% have become CEO.

Most of the time these seconds-in-command are talented, energetic, and assertive—they've earned their chance to run the show. So why is it that so many fail? The primary reason is the #2's inability to navigate the political currents that buffet every heir apparent. Two cases exemplify the problems.

A new senior vice president takes a job at an electronics company with the understanding that he will succeed the CEO. He and the CEO meet at least weekly for the first 12 months, discussing virtually every decision. The CEO agrees with all the moves and even compliments the SVP for making some tough calls. Fourteen months later the SVP is shocked to learn that he has been fired. He discovers that two other SVPs, with whom the CEO had long-standing relationships, had undermined him. Their complaint: he was moving too fast in areas that threatened their power bases.

The financial services division of a Fortune 500 company posts impressive results—in fact, it's the only part of the corporation that is growing. The division's president, who is in line to succeed the CEO of the parent company, decides that her division needs broader distribution channels. Exploring potential strategic alliances, she concludes that her division could achieve even more impressive growth by bringing in another company as a minority owner. But one month after presenting her analysis to the CEO, the division president is fired—

labeled disloyal for suggesting that the parent company reduce its ownership stake.

It's not enough to have strong managerial skills and the ability to create a compelling vision for the organization. To navigate the political minefield of leadership transitions, an aspiring CEO must *build coalitions.* Once in the #2 spot and poised to move to the top, they must accurately diagnose the political landscape. Then they need to create a critical mass of support among company leaders for your vision of where the organization needs to go. Typically, successful seconds-in-command demonstrate the following political skills:

They build a good working relationship with the CEO, recognizing that he holds the keys to the top job.

They help their peers succeed, even if some of these colleagues are also competing for the CEO's job. This shows the CEO and the board of directors that the #2 possesses the maturity and self-confidence necessary for the top position. It also builds "relationship capital" among the peer group.

They reach out to influential middle managers across the company and make decisions with their needs in mind. By cultivating support among the ranks of middle management, successful seconds-in-command can avoid having their initiatives undercut.

They build credibility by attacking problems that are important to the business and by addressing issues that employees care about. They make the tough, sometimes unpopular calls that employees realize are necessary for success. But they also know which changes not to push for before they get to the top—those that threaten the legacy of the CEO or the future of her loyal supporters.

They don't disparage the current culture or those who created it, even if their mandate is to change the organization in fundamental ways.

A company's human-resources executives, its board of directors, even its CEO are rarely in a position to make the succession work. In the end, the aspiring CEO must take responsibility for making the transfer of power work. No one pays the price of a failed succession like the successor himself. He must own the problem—as well as its solution.

Reprint U0012D

About the Contributors

Jim Biolos is a contributor to *Harvard Management Update*.

Tom Brown is a contributor to *Harvard Management Update*.

Rebecca M. Saunders is a freelance writer based in New York City.

David Stauffer is a Red Lodge, Mont.-based writer.

Jim Billington is a contributor to *Harvard Management Update*.

Monci J. Williams is a contributor to *Harvard Management Update*.

Constantine von Hoffman is a contributor to *Harvard Management Update*.

Susan G. Parker is a freelance reporter living and working in Cambridge, Mass.

Dan Ciampa, an advisor to business leaders, and **Michael Watkins,** an associate professor at Harvard Business School, are the co-authors of *Right From from the Start: Taking Charge in a New Leadership Role* (Harvard Business School Press, 1999).

Harvard Business Review Paperback Series

The Harvard Business Review Paperback Series offers the best thinking on cutting-edge management ideas from the world's leading thinkers, researchers, and managers. Designed for leaders who believe in the power of ideas to change business, these books will be useful to managers at all levels of experience, but especially senior executives and general managers. In addition, this series is widely used in training and executive development programs.

Books are priced at $19.95 U.S.
Price subject to change.

Title	Product #
Harvard Business Review **Interviews with CEOs**	3294
Harvard Business Review on **Advances in Strategy**	8032
Harvard Business Review on **Becoming a High Performance Manager**	1296
Harvard Business Review on **Brand Management**	1445
Harvard Business Review on **Breakthrough Leadership**	8059
Harvard Business Review on **Breakthrough Thinking**	181X
Harvard Business Review on **Building Personal and Organizational Resilience**	2721
Harvard Business Review on **Business and the Environment**	2336
Harvard Business Review on **Change**	8842
Harvard Business Review on **Compensation**	701X
Harvard Business Review on **Corporate Ethics**	273X
Harvard Business Review on **Corporate Governance**	2379
Harvard Business Review on **Corporate Responsibility**	2748
Harvard Business Review on **Corporate Strategy**	1429
Harvard Business Review on **Crisis Management**	2352
Harvard Business Review on **Culture and Change**	8369
Harvard Business Review on **Customer Relationship Management**	6994
Harvard Business Review on **Decision Making**	5572
Harvard Business Review on **Effective Communication**	1437

To order, call 1-800-668-6780, or go online at www.HBSPress.org

Title	Product #
Harvard Business Review on **Entrepreneurship**	9105
Harvard Business Review on **Finding and Keeping the Best People**	5564
Harvard Business Review on **Innovation**	6145
Harvard Business Review on **Knowledge Management**	8818
Harvard Business Review on **Leadership**	8834
Harvard Business Review on **Leadership at the Top**	2756
Harvard Business Review on **Leading in Turbulent Times**	1806
Harvard Business Review on **Managing Diversity**	7001
Harvard Business Review on **Managing High-Tech Industries**	1828
Harvard Business Review on **Managing People**	9075
Harvard Business Review on **Managing the Value Chain**	2344
Harvard Business Review on **Managing Uncertainty**	9083
Harvard Business Review on **Managing Your Career**	1318
Harvard Business Review on **Marketing**	8040
Harvard Business Review on **Measuring Corporate Performance**	8826
Harvard Business Review on **Mergers and Acquisitions**	5556
Harvard Business Review on **Motivating People**	1326
Harvard Business Review on **Negotiation**	2360
Harvard Business Review on **Nonprofits**	9091
Harvard Business Review on **Organizational Learning**	6153
Harvard Business Review on **Strategic Alliances**	1334
Harvard Business Review on **Strategies for Growth**	8850
Harvard Business Review on **The Business Value of IT**	9121
Harvard Business Review on **The Innovative Enterprise**	130X
Harvard Business Review on **Turnarounds**	6366
Harvard Business Review on **What Makes a Leader**	6374
Harvard Business Review on **Work and Life Balance**	3286

Harvard Business Essentials

In the fast-paced world of business today, everyone needs a personal resource—a place to go for advice, coaching, background information, or answers. The Harvard Business Essentials series fits the bill. Concise and straightforward, these books provide highly practical advice for readers at all levels of experience. Whether you are a new manager interested in expanding your skills or an experienced executive looking to stay on top, these solution-oriented books give you the reliable tips and tools you need to improve your performance and get the job done. Harvard Business Essentials titles will quickly become your constant companions and trusted guides.

These books are priced at $19.95 U.S., except as noted.
Price subject to change.

Title	Product #
Harvard Business Essentials: **Negotiation**	1113
Harvard Business Essentials: **Managing Creativity and Innovation**	1121
Harvard Business Essentials: **Managing Change and Transition**	8741
Harvard Business Essentials: **Hiring and Keeping the Best People**	875X
Harvard Business Essentials: **Finance**	8768
Harvard Business Essentials: **Business Communication**	113X
Harvard Business Essentials: **Manager's Toolkit ($24.95)**	2896
Harvard Business Essentials: **Managing Projects Large and Small**	3213
Harvard Business Essentials: **Creating Teams with an Edge**	290X

The Results-Driven Manager

The Results-Driven Manager series collects timely articles from *Harvard Management Update* and *Harvard Management Communication Letter* to help senior to middle managers sharpen their skills, increase their effectiveness, and gain a competitive edge. Presented in a concise, accessible format to save managers valuable time, these books offer authoritative insights and techniques for improving job performance and achieving immediate results.

These books are priced at $14.95 U.S.
Price subject to change.

Title	Product #
The Results-Driven Manager: **Face-to-Face Communications for Clarity and Impact**	3477
The Results-Driven Manager: **Managing Yourself for the Career You Want**	3469
The Results-Driven Manager: **Presentations That Persuade and Motivate**	3493
The Results-Driven Manager: **Teams That Click**	3507
The Results-Driven Manager: **Winning Negotiations That Preserve Relationships**	3485

Readers of the Results-Driven Manager series find the following Harvard Business School Press books of interest.

If you find these books useful:	You may also like these:
Presentations That Persuade and Motivate	Working the Room (8199)
Face-to-Face Communications for Clarity and Impact	HBR on Effective Communication (1437) HBR on Managing People (9075)
Winning Negotiations That Preserve Relationships	HBR on Negotiation (2360) HBE Guide to Negotiation (1113)
Teams That Click	The Wisdom of Teams (3670) Leading Teams (3332)
Managing Yourself for the Career You Want	Primal Leadership (486X) Leading Quietly (4878) Leadership on the Line (4371)

How to Order

Harvard Business School Press publications are available worldwide from your local bookseller or online retailer.
You can also call

1-800-668-6780

Our product consultants are available to help you
8:00 a.m.–6:00 p.m., Monday–Friday, Eastern Time.
Outside the U.S. and Canada, call: 617-783-7450
Please call about special discounts for quantities greater than ten.

You can order online at

www.HBSPress.org